Praise

Finding Freedom Through Achieving Christ-Consciousness

"I love what you have written . . . [it comes] straight from your heart, and I am deeply moved spiritually. All this resonates with me so very strongly that I am moved to tears of beauty as I read the words and my spirit knows of what you tell . . . it is a Home or a Sanctuary space . . . sacred . . . full of reverence and of the deepest silence as best I can tell with words that truly fail to describe . . . Simply to say . . . yes."

—**Trude Scharff**

Praise for *The Ego-Less SELF*
also by Cardwell C. Nuckols

"I loved this book. I was attracted to read it as a result of being an attendee of one of CC's workshops. Let me just say that I couldn't take my eyes off Dr. Nuckols in the sense that he moved and spoke so fluidly that the only way I can describe my experience is that it was as though I was observing a work of art in motion; he simply radiated peace and serenity to a degree that I had never before witnessed. This book, for me, did not disappoint. It contains so much relevant and relatable life experience and wisdom, along with helpful suggestions that anyone wanting to move beyond the ego's self-sabotaging patterns of thinking and behaving will appreciate. Simply stated, I couldn't put it down. Thank you, CC. Your words have changed me forever."

—**Lucretia McDermott**

"I met you last year at governor's conference and I really enjoyed your lectures. A lot of what you said resonated with me and was a good reminder to me. I just wanted to let you know I really enjoyed your book *The Ego-Less Self*. I read it at a time when I was struggling at work. It really helped my approach with how I handled my work situation. Being more loving rather than angry and recognizing I created the situation and trying to understand the lessons learned from the situation. Thank you for writing such a wonderful book."

—**Elizabeth Jaclyn**

"I am reading the book *The Ego-Less Self* by Cardwell C. Nuckols. I am learning that 'when we (I) don't reinforce old negative ways of thinking, feeling, and behaving we (I) can build new neural pathways that can guide my future thinking, feeling, and behavior (which all are connected).' This combined with relentless efforts to let go of trying to fix, manage, and control people/relationships, I am finding peace and much happiness on this journey to strip my ego and 'move back to the nonlinear state of where things just work out as they are meant to and we (I) can live in peace.' I am learning that most of my turmoil and battles in life have one thing in common—my ego!"

—**Melissa Estep**

Finding Freedom Through *Illumination*

ACHIEVING CHRIST-CONSCIOUSNESS

Cardwell C. Nuckols, PhD

Dear Mary!
May God Bless
you & your Journey ~
C. C.

Health Communications, Inc.
Deerfield Beach, Florida

www.hcibooks.com

All biblical quotes are from the following publication: Lamsa, George. *The Modern New Testament* (from the Aramaic). Lightning Source, Inc., LaVergne, TN, 2001.

Library of Congress Cataloging-in-Publication Data
is available through the Library of Congress

Publisher: Health Communications, Inc.
3201 S.W. 15th Street
Deerfield Beach, FL 33442–8190

Cover image ©Big Stock Photo
Additional interior photos of waterfalls by Jackie Lynn Evans (Jackiethehiker@gmail.com)
Interior illustrations by Larissa Hise Henoch
Cover and interior design by Lawna Patterson Oldfield

To my wife, Susan, and
my son, Camden;

To my sister, Jan—the nicest
person I have ever met;

To my friends and fellow seekers
John Richardson and Andy Pace;

And to Chris Ziglifa,
who truly loves our veterans.

Contents

And Jesus answered and said to them,

A physician is not needed for those who are well,

But for those who are seriously sick.

I have not come to call the righteous,

But the sinners to repentance.

—Luke 5:31–32

Acknowledgments

My life is so full of special people. Thanks to the staff at HCI Books and especially to Allison Janse for her kindness and direction in the development of this book. To Gary Seidler for his friendship and support of my work. To Suzanne Smith and Lorrie Keip—good friends are of the greatest value. To Peter Vegso, who continuously gives me a chance, as this is my third book with HCI. Finally, to my editor Carol Rosenberg, whose masterful work makes my often incongruent thoughts come to life. I think you are the greatest.

Preface

It has been over seven years since, by the grace of God, I became one with the Light. Over this time, the experience has deepened. This book is a reflection of this expansion. My last book, *The Ego-Less SELF: Finding Peace and Tranquility Beyond All Understanding,* was written four years ago. It mostly explored the demise of the ego and the experience of enlightenment. This new book looks much more deeply at the realization of Christ-consciousness (also called enlightenment, satori, kensho, samadi, moksha, among others). It is written from a Contemplative Christian perspective although many other spiritual traditions are highlighted.

In the New Testament, Jesus Christ taught and demonstrated to us that there is a Christ inside all of us. In the Sermon on the Mount, He showed us the way. The beatitudes—Jesus's set of teachings from the Sermon on the Mount—go against all the ego holds dear. It is a map, but, as you know, the way (map) is not the territory. Grace can only be bestowed by a loving God.

This book is not meant to be a religious commentary. It is a very spiritual book filled with a "knowingness" arrived at by the experience of this and other lifetimes and fulfilled in contemplation, meditation, silence, solitude, and prayer. I do not ask you to believe anything I might say. Test it out for yourself, and, if it works, keep it.

May God's blessing be with you on your personal journey toward Christ-consciousness. There is no destination, as it is revealed in the beauty of each and every moment. It is always there for you. The journey is to realize its existence and let the Presence live life through you and "straighten out the highways."

The use of male pronouns generally refer to both genders. I mean no disrespect and use the masculine out of convenience and ease of reading.

On several occasions I speak of the spiritual program of Alcoholics Anonymous and the 12-Step program. I am also referring to all such self-help programs, including Narcotics Anonymous, Gamblers Anonymous, Overeaters Anonymous, Sex Addicts Anonymous, and so on.

There is one God and everything is an extension of He who created us. The terms *God, Christ-consciousness, Holy Spirit, Self,* and *Presence* are often used interchangeably.

HERE IS EVERYTHING; YOU JUST HAVE TO FIND IT.

Introduction

"THIS IS THE SACRED UNIVERSE, IN WHICH HUMANITY HAS
LIVED AS FAR AS WE KNOW FROM THE BEGINNING OF HISTORY,
AND WHICH HAS BEEN COMPLETELY DEMOLISHED BY THE
WESTERN, SCIENTIFIC WORLD. EVERY TRACE OF SACREDNESS
HAS BEEN REMOVED FROM LIFE, SO THAT 'WESTERN MAN' FINDS
HIMSELF IN A UNIVERSE IN WHICH BOTH HUMAN EXISTENCE
AND NATURE HAVE BEEN DEPRIVED OF ANY ULTIMATE MEANING."
—Bede Griffiths, *Essential Writings*

Many years ago, I lived in the beautiful beach community of New Smyrna Beach, Florida. It is a quiet beach where one can find solitude and only the sounds of nature. The most important annual event occurs when the giant female loggerhead sea turtle struggles ashore to lay her eggs.

Loggerhead sea turtles spend their entire lives in the ocean's salty water. Driven by powerful forces of nature, they lumber onto shore for a brief period of time to lay their eggs. The mother makes her nest in the sand above the high-tide mark. For eighty days, the eggs lay buried, waiting for that night when everything changes for the young developing turtles.

After the newborns break through their shells, they are guided by some innate sense—probably light reflecting off the water. This sense leads them on an exhausting march toward the ocean. For many, this is a death march as predators or the elements end their short lives.

Upon hatching, the young turtles are approximately 4.6 cm (1.8 inches) long and weigh around 20 grams (0.7 ounces). Each turtle will lose around 20 percent of its body weight while desperately moving toward the sea. Once in the water, the baby loggerheads will swim for twenty hours to their new home in the ocean. Navigation is provided by the interaction of an ironlike chemical in their brains called magnetite with the earth's electromagnetic field.

I can vividly remember the wonder of seeing these little living creatures as they fought their way out of the nest and sped toward home—the ocean—as fast as their little legs would allow. Over the dips and rises in the sand and tossed around by the incoming tides, I was witness to one of nature's epic struggles toward the unknown but intuitively recognized home.

Think of that little turtle trapped in its eggshell. At this point in the developing turtle's life, it is the whole world—its food supply, exploratory boundaries, and all of its stimulation. The little turtle lives in darkness and probably, as far as the turtle knows, could live this way forever. However, there is something beyond, causing the turtles to fight, to struggle, and to leave the captivity of their dark, enclosed world. At some point, the struggle leads to the first crack in the shell. After more effort, the young loggerhead experiences light for the first time.

What must be going on in that tiny turtle's mind when it first realizes there is something out there much greater than the small, dark enclosed world it had grown accustomed to? I don't know if or to what degree the young turtle can comprehend this magnificence, but I am sure the turtle's little brain must be firing as hard and fast as possible.

The force of nature that propels the turtle out of its shell and toward the ocean is the same force that urges the unborn child forward and out of the womb. It, too, knows nothing of the outside world and now is bombarded with harsh sensory input—bright lights, loud noise, and frenetic movement.

As the child grows, it has a different capacity than the baby turtle. The child develops a conscious awareness of its world, allowing it to think—to form opinions, prejudices, and perspectives. Because it is so teachable, it is easily conditioned. Parents, teachers, religion, culture, and nationality teach the child what to believe, what to like, what to dislike, what is good, and what is evil. The child's mind becomes a product of its environment with little ability to understand the good advice from the bad suggestion. The child's mind becomes inured. This conditioning helps form the ego. It is not who you are, but what you have come to believe about yourself and the world you live in. It is this illusion of self and world that we must overcome to discover that which we really are—our true Self.

As we grow older, all that most of us comprehend about the world comes from the parameters placed upon us by this conditioning. We do not grasp our being as limitless possibility. We go through life accepting our own concepts of reality and our own self-imposed limitations. We live inside the shell of our mind.

Our shell is a one-half-inch-thick bony structure very similar in nature and composition to the turtle's shell. As long as we live within the shell, we cannot experience the glory God created in this limitless universe. The mind knows nothing beyond its self-imposed boundaries.

Unfortunately, most people live a life full of barriers, walls, and limitations. They are locked within the prison of their mind. A few feel a rustling, a stirring that moves them to ask, *Is there something more? Is there more to life than eating and sleeping, getting up in the morning and going to work, and coming home in the evening as the sun goes down? Is there something more than mind-numbing television shows, the evening's awful news, and texting and talking on my not always so smart "smart" phone? Why am I here? What is God's plan for me?*

Once you start to open your mind and peer outside the confines of your conditioning, you find there is beauty, joy, and wisdom. All of this is there for you and me to experience. God said to Abraham, "For all the land that thou seest, to thee I will give it and thy seed forever." It is all ours—not to possess or to own but for our pleasure. God has never put a price tag on any of His creation.

Actually we own nothing. It is all God's creation. If one were to buy a Rembrandt for millions and millions of dollars, the Rembrandt owns you because of the attachment of possession. It can be stolen or lost in a fire, and, when you die, you cannot take it with you. As a matter of fact, the only thing you take with you after your body ceases to function is the spiritual consciousness you have acquired over all your soul's journeys.

Do not lay up for yourselves treasures buried in the ground,
A place where rust and moth destroy,
And where thieves break through and steal.
But lay up for yourselves a treasure in heaven,
Where neither rust nor moth destroy,
And where thieves do not break through and steal.
For where your treasure is,
There also is your heart.

—MATTHEW 6:19–21

I spend a large part of my life in airplanes. At 36,000 feet with a clear sky, the magnificence of God's creation shines forth in its entire splendor. We can see the brilliance of the design. We can watch the plains turning into the foothills and the foothills into the majestic mountains in all their power and splendor. We can observe streams running into rivers and the rivers into the seven seas.

Spiritual consciousness is like climbing one of these magnificent mountains. The higher we climb, the more the scenery changes. When we see the relationship of all things to each other, our worldview loses its limitations. We learn we are not limited by this three-pound hunk of gelatinous meat in our head called the brain. We are not limited to our bodies. We are "One" with everything and everyone—*"All that you can see is yours."* This is not necessarily with our eyes but by becoming open and aware of the spiritual realm called God or Christ-consciousness.

As a neurobiologist, I cannot adequately explain to you how the brain can create conscious awareness. As a scientist, my intellectual curiosity asks the question, "How does the brain create consciousness? How can I be aware you are there and I am here? How can I be aware of all the beauty around me and speak with you regarding this world we live in?" There are any number of theories, including first-order theory, neuronal global workspace theory, information integration theory, and higher-order theories of conscious awareness. These and other theories involve emphasis on various areas of the brain such as the frontal and parietal lobes.

As a spiritualist, the answer is an easy one. The brain does not create consciousness or Light; it is the other way around. Everything in the physical universe we call real—the brain, trees, tables, etc.—is created by Light energy. Light absorbed by plant life accounts for the production of all of the oxygen and carbohydrates on our planet. Without Light, there would be no human existence and no world within which to live.

So, what is nonlinear, invisible, and immaterial creates the material world and everything in it. Everything is created by the Light and is a manifestation of the Light. Therefore, there is no duality, just Light (the universal metaphor for God) expressing itself in various forms, some of which are visible and some of which are not. Everything is Light energy. We are children of the Light.

Take heed, therefore, lest the light which is in you be darkness.
If your whole body is lighted, and there is no part in it dark,
The whole of it will give light,
Just as a lamp gives you light with its shining.

LUKE 11:35–36

We can stay within the limited confines of our conditioning and live lives of quiet desperation. However, there is another choice. We do not live in time or space but in spiritual consciousness. We can expand our consciousness—there is no boundary as it is limitless.

The Wisdom of God can reveal Itself to anyone just as It did to Paul on the road to Damascus, to the sages and mystics, the desert fathers of Egypt, and by grace to all who have been willing to give their life to the search for Christ-consciousness. On February 2, 2007, I received the Light of Christ-consciousness. My story is told in my last book *The Ego-Less SELF: Finding Peace and Tranquility Beyond All Understanding* and is summarized in Chapter 7 of this book.

Remember, all of the beauty and wisdom of all time is available to those who are willing and dedicated enough to follow the narrow road. All the riches of this universe are all there for the one who is willing to climb the mountain toward Christ-consciousness. You can only persevere and put in the effort, hoping and praying for the grace of God to bring you Home.

You might ask, "What is Christ-consciousness?" or "How might I acquire this gift?" Christ-consciousness cannot be acquired as you already have it. It is a matter of realization (illumination). Jesus showed us the way in Matthew 5–7—The Sermon on the Mount. More specifically, He gave us the map. It is called the beatitudes.

Haven't you felt the calling? You know there is something greater than living in this day-to-day world of the ego. We are here for a reason. Climbing the mountain toward Christ-consciousness takes an incredible amount of dedication and perseverance. It is a very narrow road, and there are few on it. It has to not only be the most important thing in your life but also the only thing worth existing for. The climb is for those who thirst for Truth and understand selfless service as a profound sense of joy. To take the most important journey of your life, you have to divert focus from the experience of the five senses and look inward.

We all have natures and talents. For some, it is performing service to others. To others, it is to teach. When we pursue this urge—this longing—to achieve our full Self in Christ, we also fulfill our true nature and true mission in this world. To achieve our "calling," we must move beyond our conditioning and become open to the infinite nature of God, who is universal intelligence.

Everyone is looking for it, but it cannot be acquired. Like all true spiritual gifts, it comes to you when your mind is orderly and conditions are right. I am speaking of love—not what society views as love (possession, lust, pleasure, control), but unconditional love. This is the kind of love that has no price tag and is given completely without motive. It is not a feeling but a way of being in the world. When one unconditionally loves, there is no separation and no personal realization of unconditional love. You are it, and it just is.

Love and beauty are inseparable. As long as one is looking for love, it can never be found. The looking brings in time and is about becoming. In other words, "If I do so and so, I will find love (in the future)." Love is in the moment. It is everywhere and in everything. It is in the beauty of the waves rolling endlessly onto a beach. It is in the deer I am watching in my backyard. It is even in the most evil or wretched people who cannot see it in themselves.

Do you remember when you were a child and had "the feeling"? That feeling is love: watching butterflies, squinting in the sunlight as it dances on the leaves, and chasing fireflies well into the night. How did we lose this feeling? Fortunately, it is always available to us. Just stop, look, listen, and feel the moment. This is love. This is meditation.

Notice that when you have the "feeling"—the love for all of the beauty around you—there is no conflict. No hate, jealousy, envy, prejudice, greed, or anger is possible when an orderly, moral mind experiences the moment—the love of life and the beauty residing in all God's perfect creation. An orderly mind experiences little or no "chatter," and a moral mind concerns itself with what is good for others. This creates a quiet calmness that opens us up to the experience of that greater-than-ourselves understanding and to know that this awareness is to be used for service to the world.

Yes, the world is perfect and you are perfect—perfectly where you need to be to learn the lessons you were sent here to learn in this lifetime.

This book is an attempt to move deeper into the presence of Christ-consciousness. You already have this consciousness, so there is no need to try to acquire it. The best way, I believe, is to put you in the best possible attitude to receive God's grace. Just remember, the only difference between all of us is the level of realization of the existence of Christ-consciousness. This consciousness is what Jesus the man received when he became the Christ—the perfect man. This is our destiny . . . to bring forth the Light in ourselves in order to reduce the amount of darkness in our world.

Part One
Reality

Chapter One

The Sacred

The Word was in the beginning,
And that very Word was with God,
And God was that Word
The same was in the beginning with God
Everything came to be by his hand;
And without him not even one
Thing that was created came to be.
The life was in him, and the life
Is the light of men.
And the same light shines in darkness,
And the darkness does not overcome it.

—JOHN 1:1–14

Theologians have often assumed the Word, spoken of in the book of John, was Jesus. This confuses Jesus with the "Christ." The Greek word *logos*, the Word, means Divine Mind in action—the divine archetypal idea of perfect man. "Christ" is not a person but the degree of stature obtained by Jesus who became the perfect man.

The Word becomes flesh, and the Word becomes the Son of God in the consciousness of man. The consciousness of most men is dark, so it cannot understand or believe in the Son of God. But to those who can understand, to those who have some measure of spiritual intuition, to them the Son of God can be realized.

Because of this spiritual relationship with God, man is one with his Creator even though at some point he leaves his Father's house, becoming a Prodigal. He was not satisfied to share the gifts of the Father and wanders off from the Divine "I" to the personal sense of "I"—the ego. Without Divine protection, he is trying to make his way in this world utilizing his own efforts, intelligence, and strength. He is failing and too proud to admit it.

This is the story of the human race.

At some point, life becomes a struggle to return "home" to the Father's house—to become complete and whole again. This struggle is interpreted by the ego as a desire for "more and better" to make him feel connected again. The material world offers no solution. Alcohol, drugs, and worldly possessions may give a quick glimpse of wholeness . . . but it never lasts and always disappoints.

The spiritual journey starts when he understands that everything created by the five senses is an illusion and can never fulfill. The five senses cannot attract "living water." The spiritual journey begins when he realizes there are not two powers in the world—good and evil—but one . . . the Power of God.

In olden times, wise men and women spent lifetimes delving into the depths of their minds to examine the sacred unknown. This is the unknown of the mind and all that precedes it and produces it—the Self, soul, or Christ-consciousness.

Today, very few spend time going through the narrow door and down the narrow spiritual road. Because you are reading this book, you are one of the few who believe that to understand yourself as a spiritual being is far more important than your development as a materialistic person. What you have is of no real importance.

There is only one thing in this universe of great importance—a pearl of great value. The Truth is that one thing. It is in the pursuit of Christ-consciousness that we start to discover that Truth. Within that Truth is the perfection of God's creation.

The story of Jesus in the New Testament speaks of the attainment of Christ-consciousness. Jesus gave us a map. It appears in Matthew 5 and is called the beatitudes. Part Three of this book presents the beatitudes as a guide toward enhanced spiritual consciousness. However, it requires the grace of God to fulfill the movement of the spirit within us.

Christ-consciousness releases one from all material concerns and from all fear and doubt. Christ-consciousness releases one from the fear of death. As life never had a beginning, what we call death is really just entering another phase of life.

Christ-consciousness is "Oneness" with our source. If you first seek the Kingdom of God, all you need will be given to you. We are already and always one with God. It is a matter of realization. When we are one with our Source, we bear fruit richly. Jesus is the vine. We are the branches. God works the garden.

What if you could exist in a space where there is no time or conflict and be at peace with everything in and around you? What if you could stay in faith, in the moment in the right hemisphere of your brain and experience the perpetual calmness of mind? (See the table on page 45.) What if your belief in the God of your understanding was so great that there were absolutely no doubts that your every need would be provided for and all you needed to do was be the best you can in the moment? It is in these moments that one might hear the still, silent voice of God.

Haven't you always gotten what you needed? Certainly not what you wanted but what was required to sustain life. But yet we still spend much of our time worrying about the future, about paying college tuition, mortgages, and what might happen if you die and are not around to take care of everyone else's needs.

The present moment is never intolerable. What is intolerable is what we believe might happen in the next minutes, hours, and days. Having your body right here and your mind someplace else is intolerable. The future is an illusion, and there is no such thing as security. But think of how much life we miss by lounging in the past and projecting into the future. One we cannot change, and the other we cannot predict.

This book is largely about "what is"—the only thing that is. It is *this precious moment*, being connected to everything around you, experiencing peace, beauty, and love without motive. It is about a realization beyond the limited perspective of the ego and its misery and suffering—"what is" being converted by the ego into "what should be," "ought to be," and "could have been if only." It is about the realization more and more that your life can be lived in the peaceful moment.

You might be thinking this could not possibly be true or even achievable. Well, you might be right about the achievable part as you cannot acquire this lovely peace of mind—you already have it! It is your gift from a loving God. It is the Christ in you waiting to be realized.

When we were young, we were close to "the feeling." Do you remember when life was so vibrant? Spending so much time in the moment and not wanting to be anyone else or be anyplace else? It is a state of perfection that comes easier to the young than to the old. Over the years, we lost "the feeling." I am not exactly sure when it happened to me—late childhood or early adolescence it seems. From that point on, I looked for "the feeling" everywhere except for where it can be found.

Nothing outside of us can really, truly deliver this "feeling." Oh, we can get glimpses of it from alcohol, drugs, sex, and other pleasures such as new cars and houses. However, these feelings fade quickly and are a fulfillment of desire and not a true source of happiness.

The spiritual journey is about getting "the feeling" back or at least becoming aware of it again. It is about silence, solitude—being in the moment and appreciating all of the beauty around us. It is the realization that the world is perfect—a perfect opportunity to learn what we are here to learn in this lifetime. Above all, it is the appreciation of our true selves—our Christ-consciousness—and our connection to God in each moment.

Behold, I stand at the door, and knock:
If any man hear my voice and open the door,
I will come in to him and will sup with him, and he with me
To him who overcomes I will grant
to sit with me on my throne,
Even as I also overcame and have sat down
with my Father on his throne.

—*Revelations 3:20–21*

When Jesus Christ (God) knocks on the inner door of your heart, be sure to open the gate. When the door opens, allow Him to remove all resistance (ego). Jesus overcame the material world and invites us all to do the same.

When the door is open and one travels the narrow road, he will encounter a spiritual realm. It is sacred and is neither temporal nor corporeal. Within reveals the Presence, which is Christ-consciousness or God-consciousness. It has always been there, only now you are recognizing its presence.

As the Presence deepens, there is really nothing to do except to sit back and allow the Presence to straighten out the highways. One does nothing for or through oneself but allows without resistance for God to work through us in the form of the Presence. When you are around someone with this "Presence," you can feel his energy.

One is in the world but not of it. He is like a child—innocent, moral, simplistic, and possessing an orderly mind. The character defects of the ego have been removed and no worldly problems exist. To achieve this is to overcome the world just as Jesus overcame the material world.

Many believe this is not possible and, therefore, do not even try. Some give effort but give up when immediate results are not observed or the going gets tough. A very few with the grace of God will discover Jesus's message of a Christ within and fulfill their destiny in this lifetime. Most will grow spiritually and discover more Truth during a lifetime devoted to spiritual being. Some feel the energy pulling them from the future. Others, through deliberation, climb higher on the mountain. Everyone who asks in earnestness . . . receives.

Summary

There is a Light, or Presence, inside us. It has always been there. It is the consciousness Jesus attained as he overcame the world and became Jesus Christ. Jesus was the person. Christ is the Light of consciousness.

The path is narrow and leads to the understanding that the world is perfect. This is a worldview very different from the dualistic perspective of good and evil. God created the world, and it was good.

And God saw everything that He had made,
And behold, it was very good.
And there was evening and there was morning,
The sixth day.

—GENESIS 1:31

The age of information "buzzes" around us like a swarm of bees. Sometimes it is hard to determine what is important. Is it gossip, hours and hours on Facebook, and constant texting or is this time we should be spending alone with the God of our understanding? Being fearful of what the spiritual journey may hold is healthy. Taking an honest look at ourselves is never easy. The rewards, however, are worth every second of spiritual study, prayer, and meditation. Being in silence and solitude is a beautiful joy. This is "the feeling" we have lost contact with.

It is so difficult just to "be" in the moment. Our ego looks to modify the past along with our feelings of guilt, shame, and despair. It also loves to project us into the future where we become anxious about what we can never predict. Instead, stay in the moment and *be concerned* about the future, doing what you can to prepare yourself while praying for courage and strength. Give it a try! Just sit in a quiet room in your inner room. Quiet your mind and notice there exists no past and no future—only the silence of this moment. The moment is all there is as nothing else is real. Isn't it lovely to experience harmony and the absence of conflict?

Many believe the inner room is your heart. Some believe Christ-consciousness is in your heart. I believe the heart is the spiritual center of the body. It produces and sends out great amounts of energy and is capable of receiving Light.

The next chapter speaks of different worldviews and how they shape our thoughts, feelings, and behaviors. The spiritual journey ultimately allows us to see the world and everyone in it as the perfect creation of a loving God. Just think of the difference this will make in your relationships with others and in your own peace of mind. Instead of being judgmental and critical, you can see that people are just where they need to be to deal with the problems they need to manage to grow spiritually.

I place a great amount of emphasis on one's worldview as it is shaped by the formation of the ego. The ego diminishes as the guiding principle in our life, changing our worldview toward the original Truth of perfection. As we empty out our egoic motives, prejudices, and opinions, we create a greater amount of space to receive more Light.

• •

Chapter Two

Worldview

PAST THE SEEKER, AS HE PRAYED, CAME THE CRIPPLED AND THE
BEGGAR AND THE BEATEN. AND SEEING THEM, THE HOLY ONE
WENT DOWN INTO DEEP PRAYER AND CRIED, "GREAT GOD, HOW
IS IT THAT A LOVING CREATOR CAN SEE SUCH THINGS AND YET
DO NOTHING ABOUT THEM?" AND OUT OF THE LONG SILENCE,
GOD SAID, "I DID DO SOMETHING ABOUT THEM. I MADE YOU."
—Sufi parable

We create our lives by the way we see the world. In this way, we
participate in creation and evolution. Evolution is creation manifesting itself. We can look for someone else to change our life or we can
change our worldview. These changes alter everything . . . from genes
to behavior, cognition, and feeling. As in the Sufi parable above, we

can sit back and wait for others or we can make contributions to the goodness of the world, growing spiritually as we alter our narrative of creation.

When I am tired and not up to the creative task of developing new work material or expanding older views, I like to read mystery books. One writer I particularly admire is James Lee Burke and his Dave Robicheaux series. Dave is a recovering alcoholic and Vietnam veteran who spends as much time fighting his personal demons as he does the criminal constituents of Iberia Parish, Louisiana. Robicheaux's Catholic faith is always in evidence as he and his war veteran buddy, Clete Purcel, deal with ghosts of the past and the present-day criminal element in the parish.

In one of his books, *Creole Belle,* James Lee Burke has Robicheaux reflect on the meaning of his life. The backdrop to this contemplation is the strict Catholic influence of his youth. Burke writes, "William Faulkner was once asked what he thought of Christianity. He replied, in effect, it was a fine religion and perhaps we should try it sometime." William Faulkner was a very intuitive man. Maybe we should try Christianity. That is my view on the subject.

Whether you realize it or not, everyone has a worldview. You can think of it as your own personal philosophy created by all of the things you were told you are as a child (your conditioning), your genetics, and the learning experiences of later life. You might also call it your personal *Encyclopedia Britannica*. Your worldview is made up of your perspectives, your opinions, and your motives and operates like a set of lenses altering the way you see the world around you. Remember, it is not your eyes that see; it is your brain. It is not your ears that hear; it is your brain. One's philosophy or worldview is the dictionary and encyclopedia the brain uses to reference its personal reality. This determines our worldview and influences what we say, hear, and see. It is the lens that separates us from Truth . . . Reality.

Figure 1: Five Senses

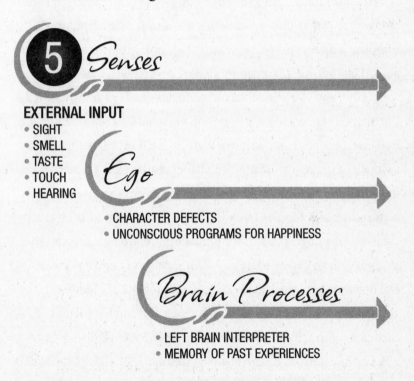

Figure 1: Worldview can be considered a story line beginning with the external senses and incorporating the impact of the ego, brain processes, and past related experiences. The ego is like a filter that takes what we hear or read, for example,

and adds to it our motives, opinions, and judgments. Early life programs for happiness (schemas, scripts, etc.) add elements about control, security, approval, self-esteem, etc., to the story line. Now this is compared to past experiences in our memory, which acknowledge or condemn the perspective we have developed in our story line. This is a conceptual model of how the mind creates illusions in the name of reality. It is "the way I see it is. . . . "

The most influential worldviews of the past and present include deism (belief that God created the world and then abandoned it), nihilism (no value to reality and life is absurd), existentialism (life is absurd but one has the freedom to develop oneself in the face of the absurdity), and Christian theism, pantheism, and naturalism. Christian theism believes in an infinite and personal God who created the universe. New age pantheism views no distinctions between humans, animals, or the rest of creation and believes all is God. Humans must discover their own divinity by experiencing changes in consciousness. Naturalism sees God as irrelevant and progress and evolutionary change as ongoing. Science is the ultimate power from this perspective.

Everyone sees it differently as a worldview can even justify antisocial behavior. On April 20, 1999, Eric Harris wore a T-shirt with the words "Natural Selection" printed for view. He and his friend Dylan Klebolt were armed with propane bombs, Molotov cocktails, a Hi-point 995 Carbine semiautomatic pistol, an Intratec TEC-DC9 blowback-operated semiautomatic handgun, a Savage 7-H pump-action shotgun, and a Stevens 311D double-barrel sawed-off shotgun as they walked into Columbine High School and declared war on all present.

Charles Darwin viewed species evolution as a capricious happenstance—a chance occurrence. His initial theory rested on three basic tenets: 1) We all descended from a common ancestor, 2) random mutations create new traits, and 3) these traits persist only if they help the species survive. This "natural selection" viewpoint is the cold-blooded process of "survival of the fittest" and the "end always justifies the means."

Evidence is now changing this viewpoint, and evolution is being seen as a cooperative venture between the organism and the environment. In fact, our genes seem to take their orders from the external environment. The dynamic play between environment and genes, called epigenesis, seeks to restore balance and harmony from the smallest level of the gene to the greater macrocosm called the universe. Nature's basic agenda is not preparing a species for dominance but promoting a drive for wholeness and unity.

As the journalist Lynne McTaggart writes in her book *The Bond,* "Nevertheless, no matter how adept at multitasking, acutely observant of change, and rapidly adaptable, not one single cell in your body is capable of any function without receiving a signal from outside of itself. In fact, scientists are now beginning to understand, the switch that turns genes on or off lies outside your body." It is the air we breathe, our life situations and stressors, the food we consume, and the people we surround ourselves with that serve as environmental switches for better or worse.

The reductionist viewpoint of the high kingdom of scientism has been under assault by the findings from nonlinear physics. As

McTaggart also writes in *The Bond,* "The latest evidence from quantum physics offers the extraordinary possibility that all life exists in a dynamic relationship of cooperation. Quantum physicists now recognize that the universe is not a collection of separate things jostling around in empty space. All matter exists in a vast quantum web of connection, and a living thing at its most elemental is an energy system involved in a constant transfer of information with its environment. Rather than a cluster of individual, self-contained atoms and molecules, objects and living beings are now more properly understood as dynamic and protean processes, in which parts of one thing and parts of another continuously trade places."

This only makes sense as God created a world that was in perfect harmony. As we gather more Light on our spiritual journey, we will attract all of what we need to move toward unconditional love and coherence in our life. God offers those who abide in Him unlimited love and harmony along with wisdom and eternal life. This harmony is the "Oneness" of creation.

As soon as we grasp this "Oneness" in our consciousness, we will realize there is nothing we need to be protected from. Because of the omnipresence of God, there can be nothing else. He could not be omnipresent and "All" and yet have a separate existence beyond the "One." Division would mean dualism and the harmony of God's creation is nonlinear.

We have accepted as a reality something outside ourselves that is either good or evil. All this disharmony comes through the action of our thoughts generated by our ego. There is nothing—no person or thing—outside our experience that possesses the power of evil or of good in our experience. Evil exists as a manifestation of the human ego, but it is not real. The ego, to varying degrees among persons, lacks empathy.

It is what goes out of man which defiles the man.
For from within, from the heart of men go out evil thoughts,
such as fornication, adultery, theft, murder, extortion,
wickedness, deceit, lust, an evil eye, blasphemy,
pride, foolishness; All these go out from
within, and they defile the man.

—MARK 7:20–23

God is manifesting and expressing Himself as our infinite and individual being. All power flows from us and through us as a blessing to the world, and no power acts upon us from outside our being for good or for evil.

All of us are different. We all see the universe in our own special way. Much of this perspective is shaped by our parents, our nationality, religion, and culture. The differences predicated upon our worldview determine where we put our faith. Everyone has faith in something. For some, it is faith in their narcissistic egos. Others have faith in the government. Some have faith in their money, their education, or their employment. All of these are temporal and pay dividends in misery and suffering because they can only fulfill desires and not bring about true happiness or peace of mind. For example, if you tell me your job makes you happy, I would ask you how you might feel if you lost your job. Happiness or, as I would rather state it, peace is an inside job. If you truly have the peace of the Presence of Christ-consciousness, you can lose your job and still be peaceful because you will know God will not give you anything you cannot handle.

Spiritual growth involves observing and evaluating all of the old conditioning that comprises our egoic worldview. As we shed the lenses of the ego, the world changes because our view of the world is altered. The world teaches us "blessed is he with a large 401k plan" not "blessed is he who loves his neighbor as himself." The world proclaims "blessed is he who has power and control" not "blessed is he who humbles himself, giving all power to God." The world applauds the ones with the most toys and not the ones who love God with all of their hearts and souls. However, spiritual growth allows one to view the world as God and to store "riches" in heaven and not on this earth where they will surely rust or be stolen.

René Descartes's scientific method perceives mind as separate from matter. The perspective is one of a three-tiered universe. There is the physical world of matter and the psychic or psychological realm of the mind, and, finally, the world of the spirit. Modern physics is destroying this view, showing us the physical world cannot be separated from the psyche or consciousness. Instead of separation, we have a field of energy constantly exchanging information (Light). The spirit is interwoven into the whole structure such that there is only the "One." Everything is a manifestation of God.

You are the Light of the world. During your lifetime, your ego has developed, creating the false belief that life is full of misery and suffering. My book *The Ego-Less SELF: Finding Peace and Tranquility Beyond All Understanding* speaks of the misery created by the ego and how to reduce the impact of the ego in your life. Think of all of the energy put into the amelioration of your suffering. The way we view the world determines how we will experience it. For example, one can look at a personal loss as unbearable misery or come to witness the experience as an opportunity for spiritual growth.

In life no one does anything for or against you. Life is a constant flow of opportunities to grow and learn. It is universal and not personal. In reality, there are neither punishments nor rewards—only consequences. We have to face these consequences to grow.

To understand this life and its consequences, let's start with the understanding of Light. Light travels at 186,000 miles per second and has no resting mass or charge. Photons are quanta of Light, and, because it has no resting mass, it is capable of interactions at long distances. At the speed of Light, time stands still. It is unlike anything described in classical Newtonian physics.

Everything comes from Light. It is the essence of everything developed in the physical universe and all of its permutations. The core of every interaction in the universe is the exchange of quanta of energy (Light). The Light of God is within you, and it is called the true Self

(Self), Atman, Buddha nature, soul, Christ-consciousness, Tao, or the Holy Spirit, among others. It is the Light in you that heals.

Figure 2: Light

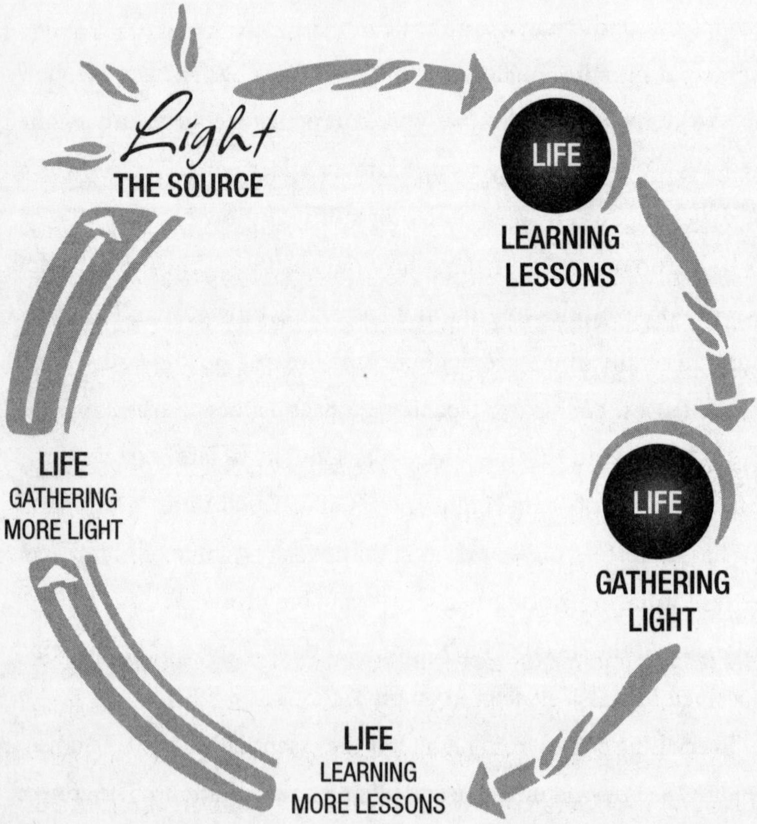

Figure 2: The Source is God—Infinite Energy and Infinite Light. After working through many life problems and over many lifetimes through the grace of our

Source, we return to the Light. I think we all have to work through the same or similar egoic problems. Addiction, loss of loved ones we thought we could not live without, depression, slavery, life traumas such as sexual abuse and rape, poverty, and other material hardships such as hunger and thirst are in reality spiritual opportunities. So are riches and all forms of worldly material wealth. These spiritual opportunities are the melting pot (crucible) where egoic defects such as prejudice, pride, greed, jealousy, lust, envy, and other defects of character are reformulated into spiritual virtues such as love, humility, gratitude, acceptance, surrender, and altruism . . . all by the grace of God.

You and I come from the Light, and our journey over many lifetimes is back to the Light. With each lifetime on earth, we start with an accumulated level of spiritual consciousness. In other words, the Light obtained in earlier lifetimes moves forward with us. With each new life and in each lifetime, the level of spiritual consciousness grows as we work through the many problems life offers us. This growth reduces the degree of narcissism of the ego. As more Light is received, the Self (love, joy, and wisdom) replaces the degree of narcissistic grandiosity and related character defects, thus reducing the level of suffering and misery.

With each lifetime, we gather more spiritual consciousness (Light) to ourselves as we work through the many spiritual opportunities presented to us. As this occurs, our worldview changes toward perfection as the ego's grandiosity and character defects are diminished. This is spiritual growth.

At birth there is no ego. At around eighteen to twenty-four months, a child develops a sense of separate self. This is an artificial separation developed when long axonal fibers start to connect the various areas of the brain. Now the child's perspective changes to "mommy," "me," and "mine." This separation—separate self—produces the ego. There is "mommy" and "me," "you" and "me," and this is the beginning of duality in the life of the child. By the age of eleven, you will very often hear a child say, "It's not fair." We then go through life worrying about whether or not we get our fair share.

In each lifetime, an ego emerges from the Self within us. The ego is developed especially during the age range of two to ten years. As I have previously stated, the ego is the source of all misery and suffering. It has a distorted worldview called grandiosity. Grandiosity is a narcissistic perspective of the world. I am only okay when I perceive myself as better than you. If I perceive you as better than me or as having more toys, I get depressed and angry. The cause of all character defects is this grandiose worldview. For example, if you just purchased a beautiful new car and I believe that I deserve a car like that, this comparison of me with you leads to envy and jealousy.

The German word *schadenfreude* speaks of the ego's satisfaction when something negative befalls another. The gossip that follows is incongruent as the person telling the story feels an inner satisfaction while lamenting what happened to the unfortunate object of the story. The ego needs this negative comparison to enhance its sense of self.

The grandiose worldview relies on something—some person, place, or thing—outside the individual to make him feel happy. This is not true happiness. For example, I just purchased the car of my dreams. I live in constant fear of the first ding in its perfect paint job so I park the car two parking lots away from my work—where fewer people park—and park it diagonally across several parking spaces so no other car can get too close. When I get that first blemish as will inevitably happen, where is my happiness? I am now living a "bummer."

On the other hand, a world seen through the Presence of Christ in your heart allows for peace and harmony in life. There is no need for external stimulation and gratification as this peace of mind, harmony, and love require nothing more. Regardless of external events, there is contentment. There might not be the great highs and lows of living the egoic life, but with the recognition of the Presence, who cares? Everything is good and perfect just as it is.

Let me give you another way to think of the worldview of the spirit. Many believe the sex act is the ultimate experience. However, for most, an orgasm seems to be more of a selfish personal experience instead of a union. This is especially true when love is perceived as an emotion and a relationship an act of possession. I give you pleasure, and you reciprocate.

For many, the sex act is an egoic biological conquest rooted in personal gain and survival. I don't wish to diminish the experience as it is a very pleasurable one. However, isn't it really intimacy we are looking for? Intimacy is experienced when my spiritual energy reso-nates with your spiritual energy. This is heart to heart. Our spiritual presence has become one in union, and we are truly connected in spirit. The eyes become glassy and the cheeks rosy, and the couple are beyond the constraints of time. It is a state of perfection, and I believe it is what we all long for. In the purest of senses, this is a total comfort and connection with the conscious energy of the universe. Intimacy is a metaphor for the union with God and "Oneness" with all creation.

Unfortunately, most do not know how to experience and sustain such intimacy. There is a reliance on external factors such as alcohol, drugs, food, and even sex to try to mimic this experience. In 1961 in a letter to Bill Wilson, the cofounder of Alcoholics Anonymous, Carl Jung observed, "His craving for alcohol was the equivalent, on a low level, of the spiritual thirst of our being for wholeness, expressed in medieval language: the union with God."

An appropriate question might be to ask, "How do I attain intimacy in a committed relationship?" Our ego complains because the other is not meeting our needs. The other is not performing as we want them to perform or look the way we want them to look and/or they are not interested enough in sex. Maybe we believe that the sexual act itself is intimacy.

What sex gives momentarily is the total abandonment of the ego. We want to repeat the pleasurable state where there are no worries, no problems, and no ego.

Intimacy is love. It has nothing to do with security; to believe so invites insecurity. Love may be the answer to the world's problems but how do we all agree on what love is? What we call human love is often related to pleasure, competition, jealousy, and a desire to possess or control. As long as you belong to me I love you, but, the moment you don't, I hate you. As long as I can depend on you to satisfy my needs, I love you, but, when you no longer are willing to do as I want, I have no use for you.

When one is compelled to love something because he believes it is his duty, he will not love what he is doing. When there is love, there is no duty and no responsibility. One does for the other because it brings him joy to do so.

Light is Love, and it is intelligence. It is unconditional and nonlinear. It is truly beyond thoughts and feelings. It is beauty and beyond description.

When what we perceive of love fails, the ego will always blame the other as it internalizes the good and externalizes the negative. It is not "my fault." Now I can develop a resentment and do whatever I want—eat, spend, drink, etc.—harming myself to get even with you. First, please understand no one or nothing is doing anything for you or against you. It is all just consciousness flowing, creating the experiences of our lives. We can choose to be a mindful participant and grow, or we can choose the opposite. We can never stay the same.

In a relationship, it seems we have an image of what the other should be and an image of ourselves and who we are. These are images and illusions. *Relationships become two images trying to connect.* The facade of the ego can be brittle. Our feelings get hurt and we get angry when another violates our image of ourselves. On the other hand, what if we could see our spouse, boyfriend, girlfriend, or lover as if it were the first time we have ever seen their smile. No defenses, no expectations, and in a state of acceptance. What an intimate change that would be!

We have an image of what we want our partner to be. Of course, we never directly share this image with our partner but somehow expect them to live up to it. Sometimes, we don't even fully understand the image we project onto others as there is an unconscious element involved.

What would happen if you created the outside world you wanted inside yourself? In other words, live your life with the openness and willingness for intimacy as if it is happening in the present. This is not easy as one has to get rid of prohibitive defenses (often from early life trauma and/or injunctions regarding attachment, control, and security) and become vulnerable and open. If you want intimacy, open yourself up to its presence. You must be emotionally available to have an intimate relationship. If you are capable of an intimate relationship, your spiritual Presence will attract others capable of such a relationship.

Intimacy is energy and not an action. It can exist when people are truly in tune and resonate with each other. Have you experienced the feeling of being with a close friend or child and getting totally engaged to such a degree you lose track of time? These are experiences that are nontemporal. You look at your watch and you are already late for your next appointment. Where does the time go when you are in the moment, totally engaged? The answer is, time does not exist.

You and I have to learn lessons about life and who we really are. With each lesson learned, we gather more Light into our lives. These lessons allow us to overcome the false self, or ego. Remember, this learning is often secondary to life's difficulties such as loss, addiction, depression, problems with anxiety, incarceration, trauma, or any of the many problems associated with living in this world. On our journey back to the full realization of the Light, we will traverse many lifetimes. Each lifetime presents us with many spiritual opportunities.

I can remember a time in this lifetime that I half-jokingly describe as my "Tom Waits phase." Waits sang with a sort of guttural growl capable of ripping internal organs into pieces (especially my heart at times). Music critic Daniel Durchholz said Waits's voice sounded "like it was soaked in a vat of bourbon, left hanging in the smokehouse for a few months, and then taken outside and run over with a car."

Waits was a heavy drinker, and I well recall his 1976 album entitled *Small Change*. In the 1977 *Rolling Stone* article "Smellin' Like a Brewery, Lookin' Like a Tramp," David McGee states that Waits said he, "tried to resolve a few things as far as this cocktail lounge, maudlin, crying-in-your-beer image that I have. There ain't nothin' funny about a drunk [. . .] I was really starting to believe that there was something amusing and wonderfully American about being a drunk. I ended up telling myself to cut that shit out."

During this time in my life, I was spiritually lost, even considering agnosticism or even atheism. The crap I needed to cut out was the ignorant belief that I was a material instead of a spiritual person. It was a spiritual opportunity causing me to lose everything I thought had value—my education, my worldly freedom, and the material fixations I thought were the sources of my ever-elusive happiness— that spun me into what might be described as my "Leonard Cohen years." Cohen, a Canadian poet, singer, and songwriter, produced a song entitled "Anthem" that served as an amalgam for what needed to happen for my life to have meaning. He wrote about hearing the birds singing to him: "Don't dwell on what has passed away or what is yet to be." The answer doesn't exist in the past or in the future. Our past memories have no power to transform us. Our fears and anxieties about the future only keep us from the experience of the moment where spiritual change can take place.

The refrain gave me this part of the answer: "There is a crack in everything; that's how the light gets in." In other words, our egos are flawed and because of these flaws or "cracks," the Light of God can enter us, bringing peace into the darkness of our lives.

There were certainly a whole lot of cracks in me. It was not God that had these imperfections but my ego. During times of distress, the chinks in the ego create an entranceway for the Love and Light of God to enter and start the healing process.

The important thing to remember is that Light is information. It is Truth. The more Light we gather as we go through our various lives and solve more and more of life's problems and difficulties, the more enlightened our worldview becomes. Your worldview determines how you think about, feel about, and behave secondary to the events of life. From your personal philosophy streams the opinions, motives, and perspectives that determine how you think, how you feel, and what you do. All of this old unconscious conditioning is not who you are.

Think about the life of Jesus in the New Testament. I believe he gave us a very strong message about conditioning. He lived in a time when the prevailing belief was people of wealth and social, religious, and political positions were the chosen ones. Jesus turned this notion on its head. He gave no consideration to pedigree or wealth. He hung around with all the wrong people, including prostitutes and publicans (tax collectors). I believe his message is we must find out for ourselves what is right and what is wrong; whom to believe and whom not to believe. Discontinue judging others. See the world with fresh, uncondidtionally loving eyes without hate and prejudice. Take everything and everyone and look at their individual merit.

See things as they really are without the distorting lenses of the ego disturbing our perceptions. A case in point is as follows. Just look at this picture of the rose.

Consider if you will, a red rose bent at the stem with the petals falling off. Upon seeing this flower, many would say that it is a worthless red rose well past its prime and should be thrown in the trash basket. However, others would see the flower as a perfect red rose right where it needs to be on its own life journey. Think of the difference it makes when—instead of seeing a person as broken, screwed-up, or deficient—we accept them with unconditional regard and the understanding they are perfectly where they need to be to learn the lessons they are here to learn in this lifetime. Really give this example some thought. Can you see how this view impacts your thinking, emotions, and behavior? The lenses of your ego take reality and reshape it in the brain to match images, expectations, opinions, motives, and past experiences.

Just imagine, if we could look at our neighbors (here used all inclusively) as being perfectly where they need to be in this life to learn the lessons they are here to learn, this view would dramatically change how we think, feel, and behave toward them. It can also allow us to be more self-forgiving as we understand this life as a series of opportunities to promote spiritual growth. Remember, these situations are not personal. They are just consciousness flowing, giving us seemingly unending possibilities to grow spiritually. Every moment, we get to choose how we will handle life situations.

When making a choice, ask yourself the following three questions:

1. Is this decision (choice) good for me but not in the best interest of others?

2. Is this decision (choice) good for others and also good for me?

3. Is this decision (choice) good for the common welfare although I might not get what I want as an individual?

If you answer question one affirmatively, it is your ego in action. The ego has only self-interest and personal gain as the basis for choice. If you answer questions two and three with a yes, your choice is driven by your heart (Self or Christ-consciousness). Let your heart be your guide.

Take for instance an alcoholic or addict coming into a treatment program. It is common to observe in this individual signs of narcissism such as grandiosity and sensitivity to criticism. The narcissistic ego views the world in such a way that misery and suffering prevail. Defects of character—envy, jealousy, greed, anger, and pride—come from this grandiose worldview. This patient presentation leads to the following question: Do you know of any psychotherapy or pharmacotherapy that can adequately treat narcissism? Maybe a dose of Thorazine, but this only works for a short period of time!

Spiritual growth and peace of mind require a change of worldview. Grandiosity sees the world as limited and constantly compares and contrasts itself with others. If the person perceives himself as better than another, he feels superior and tends to lack empathy. If he sees himself as deficient in regard to another, there exist feelings of depression, anger, and resentment. Acceptance and surrender are not possible. When we cannot accept the world as just the way God planned for it to be, the result is distress. When we try to control and change people, places, and things, the result is misery. Surrender allows us to accept the moment just as it is without the narcissistic belief it should change because we want it to. In my life, I have found when two or more people tell me I'm wrong . . . well, they are right. Usually, it is me trying to play God and control people, places, and things. I could never change anyone, but this didn't stop me from telling others how they should act, think, or feel.

These spiritual changes do not transpire secondary to thinking. You will never be able to figure it out with your mind although your whole life has been predicated on working hard, analyzing the data, and coming to a definitive conclusion. This will not lead you to spiritual growth. How can you put words to a nonlinear experience where there are no words . . . only experiences of grace? One can study and work hard to develop their spiritual Self, and I recommend this. However, the amount of study and thought is not correlated with positive spiritual growth. Spiritual experiences happen when the time is right and when we have an orderly mind receptive to God's grace.

Spiritual experiences happen in the moment. The moment is always about the unknown. The unknown—not the worn path—is the province of the Spirit. As consciousness flows, we can never be on the same path twice. We will always be taken unaware by the experience. It will always be new. Therefore, nothing can be known.

From the study of science, let's take a look at what we know regarding the occurrence of an intuitive spiritual experience. The brain is divided into two hemispheres. Each hemisphere, as it develops, becomes interested in looking at the world from differing perspectives. Although both hemispheres are utilized for just about every occurrence, over time they become more specialized. The left hemisphere in 96 percent of the population is the dominant hemisphere. It has the abilities of speech and speech comprehension. The right hemisphere is silent and more abstract and subjective. The left lives in the past and future and is generally fear-based. It is concerned with survival and personal gain and makes us a smart animal. The moment is the domain of the right hemisphere, and it is nontemporal. It is in the right hemisphere of our brains that we experience the living, complex world in which we live. This experience is always unique, always individual, occurring as a net of interdependence in a world of forming and reforming wholes. On the other hand, the left hemisphere is static and bound, creating a world of fragmented entities grouped, labeled, and categorized, which makes prediction possible. There is no link here to the subjective, the unknown we describe as spiritual. See the comparison of the left and right hemispheres in Table 1 below.

Table 1. Comparison of Left and Right Hemispheres

LEFT HEMISPHERE	RIGHT HEMSIPHERE
Temporal Cadence	*Nontemporal Cadence*
About the Past and Future	In the Moment
Focuses on Details	Holistic
Likes the Predictable	Intuitive
Language	No Language
"Chatter" in the Head	Silent and Serene
Reductionistic	Contextual
Literal	Empathic, Nonverbal
Does Not Get Context	Recognizes the Implicit
Judgmental	Deemed to Be Connected to Consciousness
Ego	

Table 1: Both hemispheres of the brain are involved in complex functions. They work in a synergistic fashion to help us understand our material reality. However, each hemisphere develops taking interest in certain functions. The left hemisphere tends to have "egoic" properties, while the right hemisphere is where intuitive experiences occur. Spending more time in the silence of the right hemisphere is an important part of spiritual practices, such as silence and solitude, prayer, and meditation.

Intuitive leaps—"ah ha" experiences—occur in the silent, non-temporal, nonverbal, nonanalytical right hemisphere of the brain. It appears the daydream state of awareness is conducive to intuitive manifestations. These insights alter worldview in a spiritual direction, thus allowing us to see the world differently. These enchanting occurrences always happen in the moment accompanied by a gamma spike of energy and a conscious awareness in the next one-third of a second. These encounters can be appreciated as they open your heart while quieting your mind. In these moments, we experience the Truth. When we are ready, the Truth is a higher level of awareness (more Light) made available to us by God. It is about climbing just a little higher on the mountain and seeing the world differently. Remember, the world has not changed, only our worldview. Each climb reduces the egoic worldview and brings more Truth into our lives. Truth is harmonious and is an experience of "Oneness" with consciousness.

Another intriguing aspect of the intuitive experience is its impact on the autonomic nervous system. This nervous system is made up of two generally competing components. One of these components is the sympathetic nervous system, often referred to as the "fight or flight" system, and the other is the parasympathetic nervous system, sometimes referred to as the "vegetative" system. Usually when one of the systems is operational, the other is diminished. For example, when you rest, the parasympathetic system is dominant, while the sympathetic system would be dominant playing a competitive sport or game. During an intuitive or "ah ha" experience, both the sympathetic and parasympathetic nervous system are turned on. This is why one might describe the experience as an "excited calmness" or feeling an "intense calm."

Table 2. Comparison of Sympathetic and Parasympathetic Nervous Systems

SYMPATHETIC	PARASYMPATHETIC
Dilation of Pupils	Constriction of Pupils
State of Excitation	State of Relaxation
Increases Heart Rate	Decreases Heart Rate
Increases Blood Pressure	Decreases Blood Pressure
Inhibits Digestive System	Stimulates Digestive System
"Fight or Flight"	"Rest and Digest"
Constricts Rectum	Relaxes Rectum
Mediates Sexual Arousal	Calming of Arousal

Table 2: The autonomic nervous system (ANS) is often referred to as the involuntary nervous system as it takes care of visceral bodily functions without conscious awareness. There are two distinct branches of the ANS—the sympathetic

nervous system and the parasympathetic nervous system. The branches coun-terbalance each other, with one being excitatory while the other is relaxation oriented. On rare occasions, such as during an intuitive spiritual experience, both systems can discharge at the same time. This is why such experiences are typically described as having elements of both excitation and calmness.

A change in worldview is what the Twelfth Step of Alcoholics Anonymous (AA) describes as "having had a spiritual awakening." The mind—analytical left hemisphere and all of our thoughts—cannot get us there, and no medications can make this happen. As one honestly and thoroughly works the individual steps, many intuitive experiences can happen. Each of these experiences will lead to a higher position on the mountain. The totality of these experiences dramatically alters how the alcoholic and addict not only see themselves but view the world.

As the Sixth Step of AA proclaims, "We're entirely ready to have God remove all these defects of character." It doesn't say your therapist, your sponsor, or your psychiatrist will do this! It states God or your Higher Power will do this when conditions are right. The step also states we must be "entirely ready." We must be totally open with no resistance, allowing God to perform the spiritual intervention. This is healing, and it is transformative, making the world look altered. Again, the world has not changed; only the way that we look at it has changed. For example, acceptance and surrender allow us to view the world as perfect, the way God planned for it to be, and to try to con-trol or change God's plan is seen as an exercise in futility and failure. Giving up the egoic need to try to control people, places, and things alters worldview and reduces our suffering and misery.

How and when do these changes in worldview develop? They cannot be acquired, and the quickest way to prevent intuitive change is to try to acquire it using the left hemisphere's cognitive abilities of analysis. There is also no technique or program that will do this for you. You already have everything. It is God's gift to you—a Christ within you—that must be realized. It is only a matter of reducing the impact of the ego, which allows the true Self to shine through. This Self is the Christ (Buddha nature, Atman, Tao, etc.) inside all of us. Acceptance, forgiveness, and surrender come naturally, and the essence of your true self—unconditional love and serenity—shines forth as you get more and more in touch with the Self. Unconditional love is not an emotion but a way of being in the world and is a very powerful source of spiritual energy. When we recognize the presence of Christ consciousness, this love permits us to become veritable healers. When we can see the love and beauty inside someone who cannot see it in themselves, this constellates the healing process and reduces his pain. Love is the universal vibration that allows for the transfer of energy from one to another.

Thou shalt not bear false witness
against thy neighbor.

In a spiritual sense, this commandment tells us to not judge anyone by their appearance. Instead, we must clearly be able to see the spiritual nature of the person. To see only appearances is to bear false witness.

To believe a person is good, bad, ugly, beautiful, rich, or poor is to not see the person at all. Christ-consciousness is the true identity of everyone. The realization of this fact is illumination.

Can you remember an experience when a child or friend came to you with a problem he couldn't solve? Have you had the experience of his solving the problem while in your presence? Do you know why this happens? One word used to describe this phenomenon is "entrainment." When someone comes into a spiritual energy field that is higher than his own, he can use this enhanced energy. It only works while he is in your energy field. An example of this might occur when someone goes to his first self-help meeting and starts to believe he can have what others in the room seem to possess—a fulfilling recovery. When this person leaves the meeting, his energy falls to previous levels, and all he can think about is using alcohol or drugs, eating, or gambling. This is why "keep coming back" makes a lot of sense.

Summary

"You have a twin brother whom you have wondered about and whom you would seek. This I tell you: he is your other side in all things and in all ways . . . Do not seek him. Do not wish to know him, but understand him.

You would walk the path of peace . . . He would not

You are kind . . . He is not

You are humble . . . He is not

You are generous . . . He is not

You seek the good in things . . . He does not

You shall respect others . . . He will not

You will seek the goodness in others . . . He will not
You are the light . . . He is the darkness
Know that he is with you, understand him,
but do not seek him!"

—*Edward Benton-Banai*, The Mishomis Book (The Voice of the Ojibway)

This lovely description of the Self and the ego comes from the Native American tradition of the Ojibway tribe.

There is no evil and no devil. Evil exists, but it is not real. It is a product of the human mind (ego). In a spiritual sense, the only thing that is real is something that has always existed and always will exist. This narrows the field dramatically!

The belief in evil is an illusion based on the duality of good and evil. It is the senses and thought (mind, ego) that creates the illusion. Everything is One and is of God and, therefore, good.

The ego is like the prodigal son—full of pride, greed, and lust—going out into the world to find happiness. As we begin to understand that happiness is not found in money, sex, possessions, etc., there is a crisis. This crisis creates an existential dread. Existential dread comes from the mounting anxiety caused by a shifting worldview. The crisis comes from the recognition one is not living his life as he desires to as a good and trustworthy person and is living a life of isolation, deceit, and misery. The realization that the path of the material world cannot give us what we long for—an intimate relationship with an intimate God and all of His creation—causes internal turmoil. It hurts when we realize we are living a lie. It is shameful to pray for goodness and to act in accordance with the egoic evil in the world.

Unless one honestly acknowledges this egoic view of the world, he will not find sustaining joy, peace, and happiness. The opportunity must be created for Light to enter. Light is Truth. Learning to live a more spiritual, honest, and coherently truthful life changes the way we see the world. Living a life of gratitude positively impacts all of our being from the way we see things to the way we feel about life. When we reduce conflict in our lives, the day-to-day beauty of the moment becomes stunningly apparent and we start to live a more harmonious life.

The ego has great confidence in itself. This arrogance leads it to believe it can solve all of life's problems by using its intellect. We have been taught by deceit. We have been taught that by using one's intelligence and the power of computers, we can solve all of the problems of the world—the environment, poverty, hunger, and war. We seem to believe that signing treaties will solve major predicaments. Unfortunately, there is no power for change in the intellect.

Remember, as we transform spiritually, our worldview alters our behavior, thought, and emotion. It's difficult to be angry at another when we understand he is struggling through life opportunities for spiritual growth just like us. How do I let someone get "under my skin" when life is just consciousness flowing and is not personal? In a general sense, no one is trying to hinder or help us—there are only the consequential opportunities for spiritual transformation.

In Chapter 3, we will look at Truth. Not the kind of truth of a mathematician or scientist, but the Truth that comes to us as we grow spiritually. This Truth changes our subjective view of the world and is the "knowingness" brought about by grace.

Chapter Three

· ·

Truth

"THE PAIN THAT YOU CREATE NOW IS ALWAYS SOME FORM OF
NON-ACCEPTANCE, SOME FORM OF UNCONSCIOUS RESISTANCE TO
WHAT IS. ON THE LEVEL OF THOUGHT, THE RESISTANCE IS SOME
FORM OF JUDGMENT. ON THE EMOTIONAL LEVEL, IT IS SOME
FORM OF NEGATIVITY. THE INTENSITY OF THE PAIN DEPENDS
ON THE DEGREE OF RESISTANCE TO THE PRESENT MOMENT, AND
THIS IN TURN DEPENDS ON HOW STRONGLY YOU ARE IDENTIFIED
WITH YOUR MIND. THE MIND ALWAYS SEEKS TO DENY THE NOW
AND TO ESCAPE FROM IT. IN OTHER WORDS, THE MORE YOU ARE
IDENTIFIED WITH YOUR MIND, THE MORE YOU SUFFER. OR YOU
MAY PUT IT LIKE THIS: THE MORE YOU ARE ABLE TO HONOR
AND ACCEPT THE NOW, THE MORE YOU ARE FREE OF PAIN, OF
SUFFERING—AND FREE OF THE EGOIC MIND."

—Eckhart Tolle, *The Power of Now: A Guide to Spiritual Enlightenment*

"No one has ever broken your heart.

Some may have broken your illusion.

Others may have broken your ego.

Thank them all."

—Mark Houston, personal communication

When I was a child, my mother told me I would need to work very hard to "become" something in life. When I was in school, I was told that I should concentrate and work hard so I could become successful in business. When I became an adult, I believed working hard would keep me from becoming a failure at life, and I identified myself with what I did for a living, thus valuing myself based upon how much money I made and what my job title was at the time. This was not living, and it definitely was not the Truth. My self-critical perfectionism kept me under the cloud of the self-talk statement, "I am not good enough."

My life—like every life—is conditioned to believe the moment is only important as it relates to the future. As there is no security in this life and no one knows what will happen five seconds from now much less in five years, I was conditioned to believe in an illusion. "I must work harder," I said to myself.

"I was," "I am," and "I will be." The "I was" conditions the "I am," which tries to control the future of "I will be." The word "I" is a qualifier (attached to an idea), and we become a slave to it. We were told we are smart, dull, beautiful, or ugly. I was told, "You are an underachiever."

Reality, Truth, or the Divine cannot come to one who is always striving "to become." One cannot acquire or struggle for that which is extraordinary. It can only come to one who is "being" in the moment with an orderly mind. It can only come to one who understands that "what is" is the only thing that is and that the future is an illusion. Now one can see that Reality, Truth, is not far off at all but right here in this moment.

For most people, there is the question of "What is Truth?" I don't claim the question anymore. From my heart, my faith in God leads me to believe in the still silent voice of the Father that creates a sense of peace in my heart and shuts down the obsessing mind. *Truth opens my heart while quieting my mind.* Many people express their opinion about what they believe is real, intellectualizing a topic that cannot be cognitively understood. Opinions are just one's prejudices and a reflection of the conditions upon which we were raised. When we live based upon abstractions, we live an illusion. Actions based upon these thoughts will be incomplete.

In what language do you believe God speaks to you? Is it Hebrew, English, Spanish, or French? God speaks without language, and we proceed to try to translate or interpret the wordless understanding into our own language. Our conditioning—especially our religious training—can negatively impact the validity of the interpretation.

No message from God can be transcribed into language. There is no language for the sublime. Our English language only describes this manifest world we live in and not the unmanifest (spiritual) world.

Even the interpretation of a spiritual teacher gets in the way as we are conditioned by our faith, experiences, and expectations.

God speaks His own message wordlessly, and we must learn to trust a wordless, silent understanding. This wordless comprehension will change our worldview and be reflected in how we see the world. There will be more Light (love and acceptance) and fewer egoic defects of character as a result. Harmony increases as chaos is decreased.

When your right hemisphere registers an intuitive, spiritual surge of energy (Light), just stay with the moment. Meditation and contemplation allow a deepening of the experience. Utilizing the mind and thoughts to create a literal interpretation will only lead you astray.

Neurobiology teaches us that the brain interprets reality. Your eyes do not see and your ears do not hear. The occipital cortex creates the picture, and the temporal lobes create the sound. Each retina has a blind spot, but you do not see it in anything you look at. It is filled in by the brain to create a continuous whole image. Life is all energy, and it is the energy waves received by these areas of the brain that become our visual and auditory world. The left hemisphere has what is called an "interpreter" function. This function strives to put all we experience from the five senses into familiar patterns. It will take bits of input and, like a computer, see if it matches our previous experiences. It, in essence, makes up things to complete the familiar scene or saying.

Since evolution has taught us to err toward the negative in the pursuit of survival, it is easy to see how we can "take things the wrong way," so to speak. Most of us can remember a time a friend told us some gossip. They may have said someone we know said a disparaging word about us. Within the left hemisphere, this one little piece of information can be translated into a full-blown conspiracy that we obsess about. When we next see that person and talk with him, we find out this one little fragment of gossip was taken totally out of context or maybe never even happened in the first place.

As I look out my window, there is a pasture lush and green from all of the rain. It is not my house or my pasture, as it all belongs to the Lord. At this time in my life, I have been given caretaking responsibility for these lovely few acres. For this opportunity, I am very grateful as we live next to a preserve, and there is so much life to experience on this little plot of land.

Two families of deer—mothers, fathers, and two generations of offspring—dine on the grass. I can remember lying on the grass to see how close they would come to me. Over time, they would come very close, constantly pawing the ground to see if I would respond. These beautiful moments are Truth and not some puzzle. The picture is totally complete as it is. The feeling of the moment and total silence in the mind create the flash of reality. The presence of God captured in an image. There is no fragmentation as it is an "I-Thou" moment. (*I-Thou* is a concept found in *I and Thou* by Martin Buber.) The base word *I-Thou* can only occur with one's whole being. *Thou* is not an object of experience or of thought. Nothing conceptual intervenes between the "I" and the "you." We merge without fragmentation. There is no purpose or motive that intervenes as it is only of the moment. Truth can only be experienced in the moment without the distortions of the ego.

There is no path to this Truth as it must come to you. To receive Truth, the mind must be empty. In this state, there is no conditioning—no thoughts, no opinions, no motives.

You cannot possess the Truth. It is always new, and, when you use time to try to conceptualize Truth, it is no longer true. Truth is wordless, timeless, eternal, and from still moment to moment.

When can we access Truth? It only exists when the mind is orderly and moral without intrusion from the past or projections into the future. When there is no "chatter" in the head, Truth can visit you; only in these moments can Truth be realized. It cannot be acquired. Do not strive, just be silent and listen for the still silent voice of your God speaking directly to your heart. You have heard this voice many times before, haven't you?

It takes a sensitive, orderly mind to hear the still silent voice of God. Fear makes the mind defensive, invulnerable, insensitive, and dull. Only a vulnerable mind is capable of love. A sensitive mind is inwardly exposed in the sense that there is no resistance (that is, no egoic defenses). This mind has no images or formulas of what Truth is. A spiritual seeker who believes he knows Reality is really lost. It is the person who states and believes, "I don't know," who is observing and discovering, neither seeking an end, nor thinking in terms of arriving at some spiritual end or becoming some spiritual being—such a person is living, and this way of living is Truth.

An orderly mind is not concentrating on anything but is aware of everything. In a state of awareness, there exists tremendous energy and great space. There are no conflicts or problems, but, if a problem were to arise, it can be immediately solved.

An orderly mind has neither center nor focal points. There is an infinite wholeness. Here, one is mindful and learning without any judgment, comparison, or agenda. Imagine being able to stay in the moment in a state of calm and silence, trusting that whatever arose—whatever problem or situation—you would respond correctly. It would be impossible not to, as this wholeness is love and unconditional love can never do anything wrong.

But when they deliver you up,
Do not worry as to how or what you will speak;
For it will be given to you in that very hour
what you are to speak.
For it is not you who speak,
But the Spirit of your Father,
Which speaks through you.

—MATTHEW 10:19–20

An orderly mind is endlessly, timelessly silent. Silence is the first language of God. This is meditation. In order to create an orderly, sensitive mind capable of receiving Truth, one must develop certain proficiencies. These skills are the art of listening, the art of observation, and the art of learning. Instead of listening with your mind, listen with your heart. This way there will be no interpretation and no opinions. In other words, no egoic observer is in play to alter the input. To see the world as it really exists is the art of observation. The world we live in is a poverty-stricken, ruthless, discourteous, character-defect ridden realm full of exploitation and greed. The inner world of most individuals is so egoic and so insecure. This leads me to mourning as I know how far I am and the world is from the perfection of the Christ. Observe all of this without words and without bringing any of your conditioning into play. The art of learning is fostered by intuitive insight as opposed to learning as an accumulation of information. With these skills, you can capture the essence of life and of Truth.

Arriving, seeking, and becoming bring time into the situation. There is no power for transformation in time—no Truth. Also, if there is no psychological time, there will be no conflict. We need chronological time so we know when to go to work, at what time to meet a friend, or at what time we pick our children up from school. Psychological time draws us into the past where guilt and shame exist and into the future and its closet full of fears . . . the economy, death, social isolation, mortgages, being alienated, etc. Remember, the ego is bound by time and lives in the past and future.

Without psychological time, we would exist in the beauty and serenity of the moment where there are no words, no "me," and no "you." Here exists the peace of God and the unlimited energy of the universe. This is where intuitive, subjective, or spiritual awareness (Light) can come to us. This takes us farther up the mountain while changing our worldview.

Just think of what your life would be like if you could always stay in faith in the moment. There would be no conflict or character defects, and you would experience the peace of the presence of Christ-consciousness. How difficult this is with the ego always interrupting those moments of tranquility by bringing remembrances of the past or worries about the future. It only makes common sense to spend more time in the present, but all of our conditioning makes peace such a fleeting phenomenon.

By the grace of God and when the mind is still and tranquil, spiritual insight can occur. When an intuitive change occurs, it happens in the right hemisphere of the brain in the flash of a moment. There may have been years of struggle leading to this special moment. This flash of insight starts with a gamma spike of energy and approximately one-third of a second later, the mind becomes conscious of an occurrence. There are initially no words. My experiences of this are of a physical presence entering my chest precipitating a sense of profound peace. In these situations, the ego will attempt to rapidly interpret what has happened. This interpretation will not be the Truth as no words can describe the profundity of a jump in spiritual energy. Remember, you have just received more Light, and you now have a greater realization of the Christ-consciousness within you.

Science has revealed the existence of the gamma spike (around 80 Hz) and the one-third second lag before conscious realization, which I previously mentioned. A gamma wave is a pattern of neural fluctuations with a frequency between 25 to 100 Hz, though 40 Hz is the usual norm for this pattern. Gamma waves may implicate the unity of perception related to advanced consciousness, although to my knowledge this has never been proven. What I also cannot prove to you is how, in the moment, you receive more Light and a more enlightened appreciation of the Truth. I believe one intuitively knows what is occurring, and it certainly opens the heart and silences the mind. I live in certainty that these experiences create a conduit where one is directly connected to the power of consciousness and greater spiritual understanding.

During these occurrences, understanding is immediate and direct. It is felt intensely. Maybe that is why they are sometimes called "ah ha" experiences.

Truth is not a reasoning process and must be discerned directly and spiritually. This kind of Truth does not occur to the reasoning mind. Truth occurs in the heart and allows for greater harmony in life. The heart harbors no judgment, fear, or hatred, but the feelings of love and forgiveness are ever present. It is this Truth of the Self (soul) that reduces and ultimately eliminates the false self (ego), its many images, and character defects. All problems of humanity are products of the material sense (ego) and are experienced through the five senses. All lack of harmony in life is seen, felt, heard, tasted, or smelled and exists in the material world and is, therefore, an illusion.

The heart is a part of us little known and seldom realized. Often, it is a crisis of the ego in the form of a loss of a beloved person, an addiction, or other life calamity that reveals a glimmer of the Self and an opportunity to move toward that which we truly are—Christ-consciousness.

The answer to all spiritual problems must be sought within. No one can do it for you, give it to you, or lead you to it. Please don't get me wrong. Studying the great spiritual traditions and working with a

Figure 3: Circles

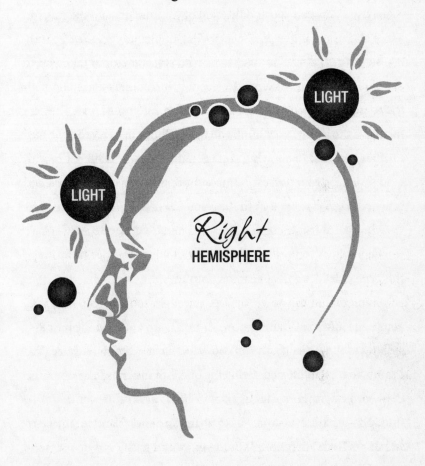

Figure 3: In the moment the right hemisphere of the brain can receive Light (information, consciousness, Truth, Reality, Holy Spirit, etc.), creating a jump in spiritual consciousness. This is the mechanism by which spiritual growth occurs in a nonlinear fashion. Remember, it is not linear moving from A to B to C but occurs as a "jump" or "intuitive leap."

sage, master, or teacher can be extremely helpful. What I mean is, ultimately, it is between you and the God of your understanding. It is you alone and naked in the presence of God, hoping for grace and Truth.

Be warned, a teacher or master who states they can take you to enlightenment and has a precise agenda, including a place and path they wish to take you on, is not capable of unconditional love. They are taking you to a place they think you need to be or in a way that worked for them, instead of allowing you to find your own relationship with God. A leader who possesses unconditional love has no agenda and only wishes to assist you in finding your own Truth. In the nonlinear world of the spirit, there are no words and no concrete answers. To someone who is controlling and insecure, looking for specific answers, this type of leader will appear very attractive.

Think of it in this way: A path—a well-worn way—can only take you to the known. What is known is not Truth and is of the past as it belongs to time. Reality, the unknown is timeless, immeasurable, and cannot be conceptualized. Believing one is of the chosen few because they have a certain master as their guide is also rather fantastic. To find bliss—the Truth—one has to abandon all ways and totally open self up to God's direction. Would you rather trust God or someone who claims to know the way to the Lord?

The answers one desires are neither to be found in human thought nor language, nor by journeying the world over looking for more and more experiences. The ego just loves experiences so it can compare one to another while getting nowhere spiritually. As the sixth century B.C. philosopher Lao Tzu stated:

There is no need to run outside
For better seeing,
Nor to peer from the window.
Rather abide at the center of your being;
For the more you leave it, the less you learn.

Lao Tzu (Old Sage) is credited as being the father of Taoism, which along with Confucianism, became the dominant philosophies of China.

With meditation, contemplation, prayer, silence, and solitude, we create the optimal environment for spiritual growth. As the presence of Christ-consciousness is being realized, the outer world will start to conform to our inner awareness of Truth. This is so very important to understand. When our worldview changes due to our spiritual growth, the outer world will be a reflection of where we are as we climb the mountain toward perfection.

This experience of internal beauty will draw beauty toward us from the outside world. Remember, all error is founded on the theory that there are two worlds in existence—a heavenly and divine world and the material world of the ego. As we develop greater levels of spiritual consciousness, you will begin to see more and more of the perfection of God's creation and less of the misery and suffering of the egoic worldview. Spiritual insights wipe away the misunderstandings of the ego, including its defects of character.

What really appears as our world is the Word made flesh, the Spirit made visible, and consciousness expressed as ideology. One cannot overcome the world when one desires to maximize earthly pleasures and minimize life's pain. Pain and pleasure are constant companions. We cannot have one without the other.

The only way to overcome the world is by developing higher and higher levels of spiritual consciousness. By realizing the Presence of Christ-consciousness within yourself and surrendering to it, you now allow the Presence to live its life through you. Therefore, don't place value on earthly thoughts or concerns. All of your thoughts come from memory—memory conditioned to align with the narcissistic nature of man in pursuit of more and better. Also don't spend your time trying to become someone or something. This is a game that never ends and is the road to self-destruction, leaving you feeling unfulfilled. Abandon the road and walk in a different direction, always remembering the Truth is already within you and the way is toward realization of this fact.

Allow the realization of Christ-consciousness to give you inspiration, beauty, harmony, and peace, leading you to love and understanding. Here there is freedom from the anxiety and fear that cripples life. Here we are divinely protected from karmic law. As the opening line of the ninety-first Psalm states:

He who dwells in the protection
Of the most High
Shall abide under the shadow
Of the Almighty.

This verse does not say everyone will be under the protection of God. I believe this means only those who are seeking to discover Christ-consciousness will fall under the care of the Lord. Later in the Psalm it says, "Because he has loved me, therefore will I deliver him" and "He shall call on me and I shall answer him." The place of the most High, I believe, is the presence of God in our heart. Have you noticed that, when something intuitive and profound happens, that we generally point to our chest and the area of the heart?

As we gain Truth, we become free. Freedom from the misery and suffering of the human ego leads to more harmony in one's life. I believe we all have a basic instinctual longing to be free. There is great energy toward completion as desire denotes a sense of "lack," as well as the energy to overcome this insufficiency.

As mentioned earlier, there is no well-worn path to freedom, but there are many phenomena one can participate in to entice more freedom into their life. The following is a summary of ideas about what might set the stage for growth:

• **Surround yourself with beauty.** Think back to the last time you watched clouds, a leaf shimmering in the sun, or listened to the song of a bird. Learn to be mindful of all of the beauty around you. To experience the Truth, you need to develop a deep feeling for life and refrain from being so totally caught up in the machinations of the mind. Rediscover the "feeling" of life. Playing with children will help rekindle the beauty of the moment and spark your imagination. The mind that is not sensitive to its surroundings is incapable of discovering the Truth, which is always existing in every moment.

• **Work toward unconditional love.** There is no beauty without love and no love without beauty. Love is the very essence of beauty. To be able to see the love and beauty inside those who cannot see it in themselves is healing. I believe if we don't have love for ourselves and for others, we can go to retreats and sit cross-legged for a thousand years and still not discover Truth.

• **Unconditional love and beauty give us an orderly and sensitive mind capable of receiving the truth.** To possess a sensitive mind, one must deflate the ego's defenses and character defects. This creates openness and vulnerability. To understand and admit that "I am jealous, envious, etc.," is Truth. Life is a process of ridding oneself of the false self in order to discover that which one truly is—the Self, which is Truth. Remember, nothing on this earth can really harm you. Giving up character defects of the ego may be uncomfortable. After living with them for most of your life, a vacuum will be created in their absence. However, it will be filled with the Spirit as you continue to climb the mountain.

• **There must be the humble understanding "I don't know anything."** The more we realize the ignorance of Truth, the more available we are to receive what is real. We are all conditioned and only a mind in a state of "not knowing" is free and capable of learning.

• **There must be dissatisfaction with the way life is currently being lived.** There needs to be the belief that there is more to life than what our lives currently hold. This displeasure creates energy for change. You may notice you don't seem to fit into some of your social network anymore. With some of your old friends, there is not that old sense of comfort. The things that used to be enough are not working anymore. The energy of dissonance gives us a newfound freedom. It is neither a freedom from anything nor a freedom we hope to gain by performing some spiritual practice. This freedom has no cause as it is the state of being free, unattached to anything else. We are so accustomed to using our will to seek freedom from something or for something. The will is egoic and is about desire and "becoming" something different from what we are. The freedom we are looking for here is a quality of the mind when it is open, receptive, and in the moment. To this mind can come freedom and Truth.

In the Christian faith, Truth is the mystery of the Godhead and revealed in the Trinity. The Trinity is often described as a concept—three persons in one. This only makes the mystery understandable on a superficial level. The mystery itself is found in the experience of Jesus Christ.

Summary

Most of us were conditioned to study hard and concentrate in order to learn and succeed in life. Unfortunately, what might allow us to learn in the academic and business arena does not work when it comes to life. Spiritual awareness cannot come to one who is striving, becoming, and trying to acquire. Truth only comes to the one who has an open and orderly mind that is sensitive and capable of receiving the unimaginable. When not seeking, striving, or trying to obtain a result, Truth might come to you.

When there is no conflict, there is harmony. A harmonious mind is orderly and free. This mind is free of motives and opinions. An orderly mind is innocent as it is not capable of hurting others or of being hurt. Only a mind full of images can be hurt.

In this chapter, we reviewed the concept of freedom and how one might receive Truth. Such things as surrounding yourself with beauty are ways of helping to establish a sensitive, orderly mind. The next part of the book will extend this understanding by speaking of how we can create a crucible where Christ-consciousness might become realized as that which we really are.

The next part, Preparation, also takes a look at the problem of thought and why thinking is not capable of advancing us as spiritual beings. Getting beyond the mind (ego) is one of the most difficult aspects of spiritual transformation. When I teach at seminars and retreats, I find most of the participants are looking for a mathematical formula or a cognitive-behavioral technique that will bring Light into their life. This is not the way it happens. Spiritual change happens when conditions are right and by the grace of God. All we can really do is to work toward creating opportunities for such a miracle to happen in our lives.

The next part further prepares us for grace. For thousands of years, spiritual seekers have utilized contemplation, meditation, silence and solitude, and prayer as means to alter worldview in a spiritual direction in order to make themselves available to the God of their understanding. Whether you are seeking a Christian God, Buddha nature, Brahman, or the Tao that cannot be spoken, these methods have withstood the test of time. I believe this history is important as spiritual seekers should choose tried-and-true approaches and stick with them.

Remember, the map is not the territory. You can follow the maps developed by the many spiritual approaches, but the territory itself will be new and unique to you. It is best understood as a nonlinear journey, not a linear cookie recipe that gives you step-by-step instructions to the finished product. It is between you and your Higher Power. The final movement on the spiritual journey is not of this manifest world.

Don't try one method for a while and then quit because something miraculous didn't manifest. Read the writings of Saint John of the Cross and see how even he wondered at times if God was really paying attention to him. Born in 1542, St. John of the Cross was a Spanish mystic and poet. He became a Carmelite monk summoned by St. Teresa of Avila to reform the Carmelite Order. However, due to friction caused by differing opinions, he was imprisoned at the age of thirty-four.

During his incarceration, St. John began writing poetry, outlining the steps of mystical ascent (also described as the soul's journey to Christ). His poem, "Noche obscura del alma" ("The Dark Night of the Soul") expounds on the hardships the soul meets in detachment from the world and striving to become "One" with the Creator. The spirit of the poem portrays the painful experiences people endure as they strive for union with God. The poem reveals that spiritual intuitive experiences in which we gain "knowingness" happen in a nonlinear fashion. They are not dependent upon chronological time but upon conditions aligning in some correct fashion.

What these conditions are cannot be known, but I believe an orderly and moral mind, the practices of silence and solitude, prayer, contemplation, and meditation as well as loving acts of service are important conditions we fulfill that enhance the probability of spiritual change. This is really a test of our dedication and devotion.

Part Two

Preparation

Chapter Four

Thinking Cannot Get You There

"Choose to be easygoing, benign, forgiving, compassionate and unconditionally loving towards all life in all its expressions without exception, including oneself. Focus on unselfish service and the giving of love, consideration and respect to all creatures. Avoid negativity and the desire for worldliness and its greed

FOR PLEASURE AND POSSESSIONS. FOREGO OPINIONATION
[SIC], THE JUDGMENT OF RIGHT VERSUS WRONG, THE VANITY
OF BEING 'RIGHT' AND THE TRAP OF RIGHTEOUSNESS. SEEK TO
UNDERSTAND RATHER THAN TO CONDEMN."

—David Hawkins, *The Eye of the I*

When I was a teenager, the music that spoke to me in a very deep way was folk music. Some of my favorite artists were Pete Seeger, Woody and Arlo Guthrie, Ian and Sylvia, Peter, Paul and Mary, Joni Mitchell, and Judy Collins. Collins sang a song written by Clannad and Paul Young entitled "Both Sides Now." Her beautiful voice and haunting lyrics cast a spell that seemed to capture the particular angst of my life at that time.

Collins sang of looking at life from both sides and noticing that polarities like "win" and "lose" are just illusions. She goes on to say that she really doesn't know life at all. From the spiritual perspective, this is a truly honest statement. We "know about" a lot of things, but what do we really know? All-important questions lead to more questions and ultimately to the mystery of that which we cannot comprehend. From the spiritual perspective, there are no opposites—no win and lose, no light and dark, no hot and cold—just the continuation of the "One" from which everything comes and to which everything goes. It is this consciousness that flows and from which everything happens. No one does anything for you or against you. It is just the flow creating the opportunities in our lives for understanding, growth, and compassion.

The word from which illusion is derived is the Latin *ludere.* This means to play with something not real. The real is what is happening now whether it is called bad, good, or indifferent. It is to escape from what is real by delving into the past or projecting into the future. This chapter speaks to the illusion we live when the ego creates the glasses we look through in order to see the world. It also sets the stage for a look at change and how we can start the journey toward the Spirit.

Can you recall a beautiful sunset with the sky full of color and the feeling that it was all magical? Think back to what happened within a short amount of time of viewing this spectacular wonder. I will bet the left hemisphere of your mind barged in and said something like, "It was not as beautiful as yesterday's" or "I wish this could last forever." Now the wondrous event is turned into a "bummer." This is the ego speaking with its constant need to compare, contrast, judge, and analyze.

I can recall a great number of business meetings where I spent an inordinate amount of time trying to predict what would happen in the meeting. First, what was the other person going to think and say and how was I going to respond? This played in my mind like a ping-pong match, leaving me somewhat anxious and disconcerted when the time for the meeting actually arrived. As I think back on the experiences, these gymnastics of thought and intellect never once gave me any advantage in the meeting and the script never followed my contrivances. The ego's attempts to use the past to control the future generally fail.

The ego is never wrong, and it is always somebody else's fault. Imagine if you will, I meet a woman who I find very attractive so I ask her if she would like to go to dinner with me (just counting the number of "I's" and "me's" in this one sentence should alert you that an egotistical adventure is about to take place), and she accepts.

When we are seated at the restaurant, I proceed to tell her all about myself, displaying my intelligence, nice income, most recent acquisition of toys, etc. Then I tell her more about myself, including how well read I am and all the important people I claim close relationships with. After this, I tell her more about me because learning about her is not important. After the evening is over, I note to myself what a good time I had.

On the next day, I happen to see this woman and decide to ask her to a movie and late dinner, projecting all of this into a later evening romance (fancy word for "sexual intercourse"). She says to me, "I hope I do not even pass you on the street again." She walks away very rapidly. If she had been very codependent, I would have had a good chance of making my plan work. Codependency is the opposite side of the mirror from narcissism. One needs to be admired while the other needs to admire. I walk away angry.

Who am I angry at? Remember, the ego always internalizes the good and externalizes the bad. How could she do such a thing to me? As I walk away I say to myself, "What a loser she is and at least I will not waste any more money on her." My ego just loves anger, prejudice, and other negative emotions. They are like gasoline to the ego. I say, "She doesn't know what she is missing" as my ego's arrogance abounds.

Well, I go to see you as you are my latest therapist. I have had so many and none of you have made me any better. When I tell you about this rejection, you have the audacity to say to me, "What did you get out of this experience?"

"What did I get from the experience of rejection? Can't you see I am angry about being rejected," is my emphatic retort.

"What was the secondary gain you derived from this experience?" you ask. Certainly there is such a gain and its name is resentment. When I have resentment, I can do whatever I want because it is not my fault. I can drink, drug, eat, gamble, act out sexually, and inappropriately spend on the credit card because *you* made me do it.

Here is another thing we can say about the ego. It is ridiculous! I am going to go out and do harm to myself and that will get even with you, darn it! Just think of how crazy this really is! The insanity is what we say to ourselves before we act. Where does this self-talk come from? From your conditioning as a child and the belief it is someone else's job to make you happy.

Unfortunately, this is human nature, and we all have done something like this from time to time. It is unconscious and depends on someone or something to make us happy. Think of the times we have done something like this. What were the consequences? Now that we know how it works and it is in conscious awareness, you never have to do it again *if you don't want to.*

> "I want to run your life for you; I want to tell you exactly how
> you're supposed to be and how you're expected to behave,
> and you'd better behave as I have decided or I shall punish
> myself by having negative feelings."
>
> —*Anthony DeMello,* Awareness

The human ego strives for control. Trying to control life is a waste of energy. Control implies comparison, suppression, and conformity. It keeps the mind from being open, fresh, sensitive, and capable of experiencing Reality, or Truth.

The ego is the mind and all of its thinking apparatus. Thoughts always come from the past and are solely the product of our memories. Unfortunately, there is no power for transformation in the past and all of our machinations will not move us farther along the spiritual path. Please understand the intellect is a wonderful thing if you are an accountant, scientist, philosopher, businessperson, etc., but to those looking for Truth, it is the major impediment along the way.

To move from the worldview of dualism and linear reality to that of the nonlinear and nondualistic requires one to get beyond the limitations of the egoic mind. This transition is difficult, especially in our world where the value of materialism is admired so strongly.

In Figure 4, the arrow illustrates what will continue to occur in the future if we see life through the lenses of the left hemisphere (ego). There will be ongoing conflict with suffering and misery. Fortunately, there is a choice. If it is right hemisphere interpretation, one resides in the silence and serenity of the moment, where there are no conflicts. Strive to strengthen your connection to the moment by increasing the level of serenity in your life with the understanding that life will attempt to pull us into past and/or future deliberations and the resident conflict.

Keep the past in the past and the future in the future, living life in the beauty of the moment. Take a moment to reflect upon your own mind and how it works. Notice the tendency to think about something

Figure 4: Past Present Future

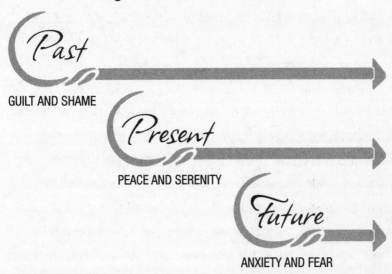

Past

GUILT AND SHAME

Present

PEACE AND SERENITY

Future

ANXIETY AND FEAR

Figure 4: Life becomes an egoic spillage of the past into the present, thus determining the future. All of the experience stored in memory, including egoic motives, character defects, and forms of conditioning are utilized by the ego to create an illusion from our past. Based upon this illusion, the ego projects into the future, which is full of anxiety and fear about what might happen. Both the left and right hemispheres of the brain receive the same stimuli (information) about what is occurring outside and in the body. Each hemisphere interprets reality from a different perspective. One of the functions of the left hemisphere is to be more analytical and to look at the world from a past and future orientation while the right hemisphere is generally concerned with the experience of the moment. Think about this! Whichever hemisphere is being utilized will determine how one views the world. Will it be full of the left hemisphere "chatter," worry, anger, fear, and anxiety that can exist when we try to change the "what is" (in the moment) into what "should have been" (the past) or "what should or could be" (in the future). All of our memories and experiences shape the way we look at something. This filter shapes how we try to control the future.

in your future. What happens when you start to think about the future and try to control what might happen? Do you notice how the mind starts to get anxious and sometimes fearful. *What will happen if I lose my job? Where will the money come from for the mortgage and my daughter's education? Will I ever be able to retire or will I have to work until the end of my life?* Now take a few deep breaths. Breathe from your heart and allow the stillness of the moment to cover you like a divine refuge. Notice the peace and serenity you experience. Are there any conflicts in your moment? Notice how one moment dies and another comes into being. It is life. We come into this world and have a series of perfect moments, and, at some point, we leave this world. There is no death just a change in how the moments are experienced.

Buddhism uses koans to help the aspirant move beyond the egoic mind. A koan creates a mental paradox the aspirant is to meditate upon. It was originally used to train Zen Buddhist monks to abandon dependence on reason (mind, ego) and to force them into gaining sudden intuitive awareness. I like to use conundrums, which have the same impact. For example, how do you love someone who blows up a busload of school children? The intellect only creates conflict as you can quote the Bible and rationalize a love for this person, but emotionally there will be disagreement, leading one to say at the end of the day something like "kill the SOB."

When not focusing on the problem and in a daydreamlike state, one might find a sudden awareness—an intuitive response—flowing in the chest toward the heart. To me, this is a palpable experience, as it feels physical in nature. There are no words to describe this occurrence, but one becomes aware of a worldview change that dissolves the conflict and allows one to truly love the person while still disagreeing with the action.

Table 3. Comparison of Linear and Nonlinear World Views

LINEAR (DUALISTIC)	NONLINEAR (NONDUALISTIC)
Newtonian Physics	*Nonlinear Physics*
Cause/Effect	Only Effect
Objective	Subjective
Language	No Words
Brain "Chatter"	Silence
Past/Future	Present
Fear Based	Serene
Conflict	No Conflict
Opposites	No Opposites

Table 3: This is a quick overview of the differences between the linear, dualistic worldview and the nonlinear, nondualistic perspective. It is easy to see how a nonlinear existence leads to peace where the linear view of the world leads to conflict, misery, and suffering. The nonlinear view is all that is ("what is") while the linear view is full of the conflict caused by trying to change reality into "what should be" or "could have been." This linear view is the conditioned ego striving to fulfill its conditions.

The ego and the intellect are stuck in the linear world of duality. There is always a cause to every effect and always someone to blame for any problem. The nonlinear spiritual world has no words, and there is no cause for anything. Things happen when conditions are right. There are no logical steps you can accomplish to arrive at some distant spiritual place. One has to get beyond the mind to access the truly spiritual. For those who like to be in control, this is an especially difficult challenge.

Thought breaks life into fragments and divisions. The analytical left hemisphere loves to label, look for the smallest part, and divide everything into nice little boxes as categories. This egoic perspective of the world is very good at seeing the tree while missing the forest, so to speak. On the other hand, the right hemisphere sees the forest and misses any particular tree. It is holistic and congruent with the world as "One."

Some spiritual disciplines describe opposites as an illusion. Our thinking perceives light as the opposite of dark and cold as the opposite of heat. In the subjective, spiritual sense, there are no opposites. How can there be when the world is connected as an energetic "One." In this world, cold is the absence of heat and dark is the absence of light. You can spend a lifetime contemplating the significance of nonlinear "Oneness" before arriving at a simple answer. There is no separation—no you and no me, no us and no them—just "isness" . . . divine "Oneness."

The ego strives to understand that which it is incapable of comprehending. In the spiritual realm, awareness is a knowingness that is beyond words and descriptions. It just is. As God stated, "I am." However, the ego tries to put into words what cannot be described. Incapable of dealing with the moment, it spends its energy converting "what is" (the actual, the moment, the only thing that really exists) into "what should be," "what could be," "what should have been," or "what ought to be." All of this is just frivolous illusion.

It is very important to understand that wisdom has nothing to do with thought. Wisdom operates when the mind views the whole as an endless phenomenon. The wise mind understands that it does not know anything. When one says, "I do not know," the mind becomes empty of content and is open, living, new, and sensitive. Truth can exist in such a space.

How can we become aware beyond the wall of the past? Can we reach a place not touched by memory or time? Obviously the answer is found in the moment. The right hemisphere is silent as there are no words. The right hemisphere is nontemporal, staying always in the moment. Mindfulness meditation and Contemplative Christian Centering Prayer are two techniques helpful in attaining this space. It may be very difficult when one starts out, and these techniques are not for everyone. Some may find other styles of meditation more personally effective. Some might choose to surround themselves with beauty or listen to certain types of music like Tibetan incantations, Gregorian chants, classical music, or improvisational jazz. The point is to spend more time in the right hemisphere. Get the ear buds out of your ears, put the phone aside, and sit alone with God in the silence of your inner chamber.

The ego is the entity that is aware of its relationship to people, places, and things such as ideas. This relationship is conditioned by the past. The whole image the ego has of itself has literally nothing to do with that which we are—the true Self. The ego is living your life for you as if it is the real you instead of a charlatan. The ego acts and thinks according to the image of itself and its image of the world. It is the lens you see through and determines how you view the world.

The ego separates itself from what it observes. There is the "I" and "you," the "us" and "them" as separate entities. The ego removes itself from any problem. For example, the ego says, "I have a little difficulty with greed, and I will fix it." There are two problems here. The "I" and the "greed" are one and inseparable. This is honesty and truth. Greed is not something you have like a cold virus; it is you and every cell of your body. There is no separation. Secondly, time as the future has been entered into the equation. "I will fix it" is a future consideration, denoting action to be initiated later. Time possesses no power for change.

The ego can only exist when it is occupied with something. Quite often it is occupied by our defects of character. These defects come from the conflict caused by the duality or separation between "I" and "you." When the ego compares and contrasts its images with other people, places, and things, this leads to *envy* and *jealousy*. Believing it is better than others, the ego becomes *prideful* and *arrogant* with a *lack of empathy*. Caught in the struggle to gain and achieve power and security, the ego becomes *greedy*. Fearing that it will not get what it desires, the ego is afraid and often covers this fear with *anger*. The conflict of duality creates a large number of conditions that add to life's suffering and misery, including:

- Being judgmental

- Being self-centered

- Being resentful

- Being prejudiced

- Being full of self-pity

- Being self-righteous

- Being impatient

- Being perfectionistic

I suspect that beneath these defects of character is the ego's need to be in control. If only it can control everything and everyone, it can maintain the illusion that it is powerful. The ego's precious images of itself and others can be maintained.

An attachment can cause conflict as it separates us from others. If I say to you, "I am a white Anglo-Saxon protestant American" (having some degree of pride and attachment to my background and conditioning) and you are from Asia and a follower of the Buddhist faith (and also have some pride and attachment to your heritage), there is the creation of separation and potential conflict. Relationship is connection. In being with people, I generally describe myself humbly as "a human being" as we all can align with the description. Without attachment, we can start to have genuine empathy for others and create the beginnings of unconditional love as our relationship is based on freedom and compassion. Interestingly, the brain can either be in an analytical thought mode or can be present and empathic, but it cannot do both at the same time. Empathic and analytical thinking are mutually exclusive in our brains.

As long as one is encumbered by defects of character and the conflict caused by attachment, we cannot meditate, we cannot have a quiet mind, and we cannot find Truth. We cannot allow what is happening in the moment to teach us the lessons we are here to learn. We stay stuck in the understanding of life as a frustrating experience.

I equate attachment with addiction in that our energy is diverted from life nourishing and spiritual growth action to short-term gratification. Life in our times dictates work and other interactions. What I am speaking of here is how we spend "our" time and making sure we create significant "our" time. To me, there are four critical relationships in my life that if nurtured will pay the most important dividends. These are:

1. My relationship with the God of my understanding

2. My relationship with myself and my personal spiritual growth

3. My relationship with the people in my life I love, including family and a few close friends

4. My career work, be it paid or voluntary, where the intention is to be of service with love and integrity.

Here is another way to think about this process of learning from the appearance of life problems (spiritual opportunities) caused by attachment. For example, have you ever felt sorrow? It often appears when we lose someone (an attachment) we think we cannot live without or something we believe is necessary for life such as alcohol, drugs, overeating, or gambling. It comes when a prison door clangs shut, reverberating down empty halls and you know you are there by yourself and all alone with no one to help you.

Sorrow is always accompanied by fear. The fear is not about the other we lost to death or the alcohol or drug. The fear is a selfish concern about what loss means to us personally. For instance, I lost the person who was always there for me or the drug that always gave me relief in mere seconds. I am sorrowful because I am losing the personal benefits of the attachment. No more person to take care of my needs or a pill to take away the distress of my life.

If one stays with the sorrow, it will move him into an existential loneliness. Here, one realizes he is all alone. Here one experiences an icy cold, blue, and lonely place full of pain. What do we do when we experience this degree of agony? In the past, we ran back to our attachments to alcohol, drugs, people, or whatever has worked for us. Unfortunately, there is no spiritual growth and the only experience we gather to ourselves is more suffering.

What if you observed the feeling of loneliness and allowed it to teach you? What if you experienced the sensation of loneliness without putting any words to it? Quickly the mind will become silent. Over time, the silence will take you to aloneness. I believe the ability to get along with and love yourself is critical to the spiritual student. It is necessary, as silence and solitude are uncomfortable to one who has not learned to truly be alone. It is only when we grow to love and accept ourselves as we are that the ability to truly have love and compassion for another comes to fruition. What a wonderful change in worldview! Instead of needing to be better than others or feeling good when something bad happens to our neighbor, we can have true gratitude for the good happening to us as well as the good happening to others around us.

What does being alone really mean? The word "being" means to not strive to be something or someplace else but to exist in the moment. Aloneness doesn't mean isolation. One is never truly alone or isolated as God is always with us and we are "One" with everything. It speaks to being alone with the world of relationships going on around us. To be alone, in the moment, despite the noise means to give up all illusions (opinions, motives, images) and see everything as if it were being viewed for the first time. Now one is outside the influence of society, and inwardly there is freedom from social disorder. This is being in the world but not of it.

As mentioned previously, there are no medications or psychotherapy that alleviates the narcissistic ego and its defects of character. The solution is spiritual. Later in this book, I will write about preparing oneself to realize the Presence of Christ-consciousness. It is Christ-consciousness that eradicates the sources of confusion, conflict, and suffering caused by the illusory ego.

How can we understand and harness the opinions, prejudices, and defects of the ego? The ego left to its own devices makes the same mistakes over and over again. By externalizing all "bad" and internalizing all "good," there is little learning from negative experiences. From a personal perspective, I spent years learning to become aware of every thought coming into my mind. You might think this fanatical, but it is an extremely effective way to teach the mind to see beyond its thoughts. Thought operates from memory and the unconscious programs or schemas we have that determine our response to life situations. These are often automatic thoughts coming from early life beliefs secondary to our conditioning. Our perspectives, opinions, and motives that shape our worldview come largely from this conditioning and are unconscious, often depending upon someone or something else to make us happy.

These automatic thoughts often contain overgeneralizations using words like "never," "always," "everyone," and "no one." As an example, Rodney Dangerfield stated he told his psychiatrist that everyone hated him. His psychiatrist responded, "That's ridiculous, everybody hasn't met you yet." Read my first book *The Ego-Less SELF: Achieving Peace and Tranquility Beyond All Understanding* for an in-depth understanding of the ego's unconscious programs for happiness and how to rid yourself of their negative impact on your life.

To accomplish this, one must become aware of thoughts as they arise. The meaning of the thought is in the past. One must get beyond living in the past to experience the beauty of the moment. The practice of listening to yourself is a doorway to understanding your opinions, prejudices, resentments, envy, jealousy, and other defects of character. When you bring these unconscious ways of seeing things into the present, you now have conscious control. Now you can surrender them to God and choose a different path. Truly listening to yourself with honest appraisal allows you to truly listen to another even when they are not speaking.

Let's look at how paying attention to our mind and its thoughts can be of assistance to the spiritual aspirant. Remember, as long as there are illusions, opinions, and perceptions based upon avoidance of "what is," you can never grasp Truth. Our life is a struggle to deal with the fear, anxiety, boredom, sorrow, depression, loneliness, misfortunes, and regrets while desperately trying to hold on to moments of pleasure. To find Truth, we must first become aware of the duality of pain and pleasure as a manifestation of the ego.

Imagine you see a car and have a sensation and a strong desire to own it. In trying to get the car (desire), there is conflict, pain, pleasure, and suffering. We want the pleasure of having the car, but in the fulfillment of desire, there is always both pleasure and pain. It is important to understand the difference between fulfillment of a desire and true peace and happiness. When you are truly at peace with yourself and the world, what happens outside you cannot create misery and suffering. It is the understanding that whatever comes your way is neither good nor bad but only an opportunity for awareness and spiritual growth.

Let's spend a little more time looking at desires as the cause of the ego's defects of character. For example, if I were a greedy man I might say to you, "I've decided to not be so greedy, and I am going to change." Well, we have already discovered the two reasons (time and separation) why this is not going to be an effective way to reduce my greed. What would happen if I experience the sensation of greed within myself and did not label it or put any words to it at all? If I stay with the sensation to the end without trying to transform it and instead only wishing to understand and accept it, my mind will become absolutely silent. Here there is no thought, no thinker, and only silence. *This silent state occurring in the right hemisphere is the most active energy state and the only creative state.* In the silence of the right hemisphere, reality ("what is") can exist, and it is where transformation becomes possible. One is connected with the energy of consciousness or Light.

Open attention creates awareness and acceptance without interpretation. If we can remain with the sensation without naming it and face the greed, anger, envy, etc., without hope or despair, we create the circumstances upon which intuitive encounters can unfold. In this silence, one is connected to the unspeakable that is the Truth of reality. Regardless, staying with the sensation without putting words to it will change the relationship and change one's awareness.

It is important to observe the workings of the mind without evaluation, judgment, analysis, or criticism. This evaluation of how one is feeling (the sensation) must be at great depth and not just superficial. Invite the sensation deeply into your being and hold it there. The desired result is to know yourself from moment to moment. This is a difficult task to learn as it takes perseverance and great dedication.

The question is "How do I end all of the conflict in my life?" The answer is to seek the Truth. Where sensitivity and love exist, there can be no conflict. All conflict will wither away if we can just quit sustaining it by continually living in the past and future.

The ego's "should," "ought to have," and "could have been" amplify the conflict leading to negative emotion and, ultimately, if not corrected, internal "cycling." Consider the following situation. Someone has just said something to you that makes you angry. Probably they have violated the image you have of yourself, creating the negative emotion. We blame them for making us angry. This is the first difficulty because no one can make you angry but yourself. Now you have a series of thoughts like, "I don't know why he did this to me. I am a nice person, and he is just mean and spiteful. This is the last time I will ever be around this awful person." Of course this fuels your emotional anger, which escalates, causing you to have more negative thoughts about the other person. This is called internal "cycling," and now you cannot sleep.

What if—after the action of the other—you didn't name the sensation you were feeling (anger) and allowed your mind to become silent? You could now counterintuitively invite the sensation into your body and after a minute or two just surrender it to God. You might now wish to objectively analyze why the other person's comment made you so angry. You will find one of your opinions or motives concerning yourself were violated. Ask yourself the question, "Where did this opinion come from and is it valid?" You will learn a great deal about yourself this way!

If you choose to try this approach remember the following:

- **First,** if you experience anger, jealousy, envy, greed, etc., just observe it in the present moment without condemning, comparing,

Figure 5: Circles

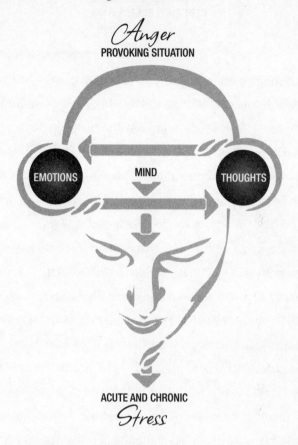

Figure 5: The mind grasps a situation in which one's image of oneself is violated. It could be gossip, something your boss or partner said to you, or even your own negative self-talk regarding a perceived slight. Often the mind will deal with something that causes anger, for example, by "cycling" back and forth between thoughts and emotions. The first thing we experience is a sensation. Then we initiate self-talk such as "I don't know why that person did this to me because I am such a nice person." Next, we experience an escalation in anger. As this continues to cycle, the emotion increases, and we often become resentful, which leads not only to sleep difficulties that night but also to self-defeating behaviors such as overeating, drinking, taking drugs, spending money, and so on. As this continues to cycle back and forth between escalating emotions and more vitriolic thought, a state of acute stress leads to chronic stress and symptoms such as elevated blood pressure, faster heart rate, insomnia, and gastrointestinal upset.

contrasting, or evaluating. Let the sensation flower and notice how it soon disappears, leaving the mind in the silence of the right hemisphere. Now you are connected to the Light, which holds all information.

- **Second,** by counterintuitively inviting the sensation into your body, you are going against your history of repression or acting out.

- **Third,** the ego is always in search of new experiences that it compares and contrasts to its past memories. These past memories are conditioned and can only distort reality. They can never be anything new and profound. In other words, there is no spiritual Truth there. For example, I have heard people describe a spiritual breakthrough with wordy, intellectual insight and analysis. This is just a manifestation of the spiritual ego. Given a little spiritual knowledge, the ego will use it to its advantage. I cannot tell you how many people tell me they are spiritually enlightened when they read my earlier book or attend a spiritual training. I have no doubt they are sincerely trying to move along a spiritual path, but they are usually trying to acquire spirituality, which cannot be accomplished but must be realized. According to the method of applied kinesiology (see the work of Dr. David Hawkins), there are probably about six people in the world who are truly spiritually enlightened. This method is controversial, and results from the scientific literature are mixed, but it is the only method that I know is available to measure spiritual progress.

- **Fourth,** just observe all of your fears, sorrows, pleasures, and all of the happenings occurring in your daily life. This observation in open awareness creates no distortion (bypasses the ego's lenses), and you can, with the grace of God, experience Truth.

Summary

It is a grand illusion to believe the world can be controlled by the rational mind.

Life is a marvelous teacher if we pay attention. One cannot run away from their sorrows, loneliness, depressions, and so on, as the energy stays trapped within us. At one time or other, one lifetime or another, we must ultimately face these apparent difficulties in order to grow spiritually.

There are many paths to Truth. (I use the word "path" loosely, as I do not feel there is a path to enlightenment. There are approaches that can be very helpful, but, ultimately, it is between you and the God of your understanding.) Generally, the three most common are the path of the mind, the path of the heart (Love), and the path of selfless service (Action). In this chapter, we have looked at certain aspects of the path of the mind, which might include the monitoring of all thoughts as a way to get to the details of the egoic mind. As each detail arises, you can choose to surrender it to God. When there is nothing left to surrender, all you have left is your life and again the choice arises to surrender your life to God. One should not be concerned with whether or not you leave this earth or stick around for some greater purpose. There is no death (no duality of alive and dead), so why worry about it? Ultimately, this can lead to enlightenment if by the grace of God.

This path is felt to be the most difficult as there are so many mental distractions in the world today. As a scientist and since the mind and knowledge were so very important to me, the path of the mind seemed the right approach for me.

The path of the mind is sometimes difficult to grasp. If you decide to choose this approach, hopefully the following will be helpful:

1. When there is no movement to change "what is," the "what is" ceases.

2. This occurs in the completeness of silence and is within the energy capable of transformation.

3. If you say, "I must get rid of my greed and prejudice," this is an abstraction and there is no reality to the statement.

4. If you say, "I must observe my greed and prejudice" with open awareness and not by trying to develop the opposite (altruism), you can find freedom. Remain with the suffering (sensation) without the words and the desire to move beyond.

5. Let the mind remain with the sensation (feeling) and not try to move away from it. The ego will not want to leave the feeling alone and will try to analyze, compare, contrast, etc. It will desperately want to rush in with all kinds of mind "chatter." When the ego takes control, there will be conflict.

6. Can you let what you are observing tell you its story without you telling it what it should be? This is truth.

This chapter looked at ways to quiet the mind and bring about greater order. An orderly mind will be of great value when we look at what I describe as the crucible for change: contemplation, meditation, silence and solitude, and prayer. There is tremendous overlap among these approaches. For example, silence and solitude is prayer in its truest sense. There is also tremendous variation in individual approaches. We are trying to create time to be with the God of our understanding. If you like practicing meditation and can create silence and solitude as part of this practice, then stick with it. I like to create times for silence and solitude. I also read the Bible and usually another spiritual reading in the morning to start the day. Contemplation is life from my perspective. There are generally spiritual concepts with esoteric meanings that come to mind at various times during the day. During times of silence, I may hear the still silent voice of God revealing a deeper understanding.

It is time to slow down now and come to rest. Make time for your spiritual development as it is the greatest concern of your life.

Chapter Five

• •

The Crucible of Change

"At the center of our being is a point of nothingness which is untouched by sin and illusion, a point of pure truth, a point or spark which belongs entirely to God, which is never at our disposal, from which God disposes of our lives, which is inaccessible to the fantasies of our own mind or the brutalities of our own will. This little point of nothingness and of absolute poverty is the pure glory of God written in us, as our poverty, as our indigence, as our sonship. It is like a pure diamond

BLAZING WITH THE INVISIBLE LIGHT OF HEAVEN. IT IS IN
EVERYBODY, AND IF WE COULD SEE IT, WE WOULD SEE THESE
BILLIONS OF POINTS OF LIGHT COMING TOGETHER IN THE
FACE AND THE BLAZE OF A SUN THAT WOULD MAKE ALL THE
DARKNESS AND CRUELTY OF LIFE VANISH COMPLETELY. I HAVE
NO PROGRAM FOR THE SEEING. IT IS ONLY GIVEN. BUT THE GATE
OF HEAVEN IS EVERYWHERE."

—Thomas Merton, *A Merton Reader*

A crucible is a container that can withstand very high temperatures.
It is a melting pot in which ingredients are mixed and melded into
something new. This new product usually has greater value than its
precursors. Using the crucible as a metaphor, we can consider ways
in which we can increase our contact with God and, in doing so,
make ourselves more available to grace. By mixing the ingredients—
contemplation, meditation, silence and solitude, and prayer—we open
ourselves up to the most amazing end product. That end is the grace
of God and Christ-consciousness.

We present ourselves in our naked, vulnerable, and open state and
ask God to intervene on our behalf such that by grace we can be born
again. This rebirth can be conceived as a new worldview, changing
our behavior, thoughts, and emotions in such a way we start to see
the perfection of God's creation.

Contemplation, meditation, silence and solitude, and prayer are all
similar. They are conduits that allow us to come closer to the Presence

of God. This closeness is an awareness of the Presence inside us. These vehicles can allow us to perceive the still silent voice of God—the Truth, the Light that the acquisitiveness of darkness cannot overcome. Oh, how difficult it is to hear this voice with all of the noise going on around and within us. It is necessary to quiet the mind and detach from the distractions of our materialistic domain.

These methods are thousands of years old. They are part of the history of man's search for the mystery of creation. Students of the spirit since the beginning of the existence of hominids (two-legged folks like us) have delved into the mind and viewed the beauty of this world and wondered about reality. Feeling vulnerable and amazed, mankind has searched for some certainty of existence that can only be accepted as a mystery. However, man has discovered ways to experience the Presence by detaching from this world and finding the silence of consciousness. It has been called many things—Brahman, Buddha nature, the Tao that cannot be spoken, the Spirit, and the Godhead.

The following is a short summation of the various ways we create an orderly and silent mind capable of receiving God's Light. I am more interested in trying to understand the concepts of the practices and have placed little emphasis on the "how to" aspects as so many books have been written on topics such as mindfulness meditation and prayer, and contemplative practices such as Centering Prayer.

Everyone has to find their own way and come to realize what works best for them. For example, one can encounter a mindful state while sitting in the silence of his meditation room or by walking in a forest, watching an endless stream, or viewing wave after wave as they meet the shore. I actually find sitting in airports a meditative experience. After so many years of flying, being in an airport puts me in a trance-like state similar to daydreaming.

You may find some of these practices more beneficial than others. All demand commitment, thus begging the question, *How much do you really want to grow spiritually?* If this is your highest priority, make time for God first and everything else will take care of itself. People sometimes tell me, "If I spend time away from my family, work, etc., isn't that being selfish?" Working on one's spiritual being is not really self-centered, as what you do for yourself you also do for everyone else. Your spiritual energy impacts those around you and the level of spiritual consciousness in general. An enhanced level of spiritual consciousness gives to the world. And remember, the hand that gives also receives. Like most things of importance such as raising your children, you have to devote time, discipline, and perseverance in order for important growth to occur. Always keep in mind, this growth is not linear but occurs in the moment. Intuitive insight happens when conditions are right. This chapter speaks of how we can create the most optimal conditions for changes in spiritual awareness to occur.

Contemplation

"When our life ceases to be inward and private,
conversation degenerates into mere gossip . . .
in proportion as our inward life fails, we go more constantly
and desperately to the post office. You may depend on it,
that the poor fellow who walks away with the greatest
number of letters proud of his extensive correspondence
has not heard from himself this long while."

—*Henry David Thoreau*, **Walden and Other Writings**

Contemplation has a rich history reaching back to Plato and Hinduism. The *sannyasi* in the Hindu faith is one who renounces the world to seek God. This renunciation goes far beyond what is ordinarily understood as the "world." The sannyasi renounces all sin, as well as the realm of "signs" (human expressions) and of appearances. Here the world of science, politics, and economics and the world of cultural life are seen as a land of appearances with no ultimate reality. Even the church and its doctrines and sacraments fall into the world of "signs"—all destined to pass away. The sannyasi does not reject the signs and appearances but chooses to go beyond them to that which is signified. To mistake the sign for the ultimate reality is considered a form of idolatry.

From a Christian perspective, one could say a sacrament is the sign of a sacred thing. The paschal lamb (this image refers to Jesus Christ as the perfect sacrificial offering), for example, does not contain or cause grace but signifies the grace of Christ. Christ brings about salvation under the cover of visible things but not through them.

The sannyasi must move beyond every human institution, beyond all religion, and even beyond all religious scripture in an attempt to find what every scripture and religion signifies but can in no way name—the ultimate unnamable mystery many call God. We might say that Jesus was a sannyasi who became Jesus Christ.

During the first four centuries of the new era, many believers of Jesus's doctrine refused to follow the creation of the church and its dogmatic approach to faith. These followers included the desert fathers of Egypt who chose to spend time in solitude and silence, seeking to understand what the words of Jesus meant to them. They wished to hear the still silent voice of their Creator. Contemplative seekers of later times include John of the Cross, Theresa of Avila, Thomas Merton, and more recently Father Thomas Keating, who teaches Centering Prayer. Centering Prayer is very similar to the Zen Buddhist technique called mindfulness.

In John Cassian's book *The Conferences,* many of the desert fathers were interviewed and the interviews transcribed. Cassian writes, "Our profession also has a scopos proper to itself and its own end, on behalf of which we tirelessly and even gladly expend all our efforts. For its sake the hunger of fasting does not weary us, the exhaustion of keeping vigil delights us, and the continual reading and meditation on scriptures does not sate us. Even the unceasing labor, the being stripped and deprived of everything and, too, the horror of the vast solitude do not deter us." Their goal was purity of heart arrived at by diligence and perseverance in the seeking of the Truth. The Love of God, which transcends the earth, abides until the end as all else perishes.

It is important to remember that what we now call Christianity had its origins as an Eastern mystical religion full of meditation and contemplation. In Eastern Christianity, the word *contemplation* means to attempt to see God or have a vision of Him. This involves an actual experience of God instead of a more dogmatic rational or reasoned understanding.

In Eastern Christianity, contemplation is described as *theoria,* meaning to have a vision of God. *Theoria* in the Greek tradition means to contemplate. It is derived from the Latin word *contemplatio,* meaning to "gaze at," "be aware of," or "looking at." I will use the Eastern Christian perspective described as a state of beholding God or having a union with God where the heart is reconciled into one thing—the Presence of God.

A contemplative believes the next world starts in this world and heaven can be experienced in this life, although imperfectly, if one surrenders his life to contemplative pursuits. Above all, Love is the answer. This is an unconditional love that increases by pouring itself into the world. This is a self-emptying process called kenosis. It is self-giving for the sake of others. Love grows by selfless service and becomes more powerful by giving itself away. God is love and resembling His love to the best of our ability brings us closer to Him.

The contemplative life is devoted to the knowledge and love of God and for the love of others for His sake. It is believed one begins to understand the meaning of contemplation when one intuitively selects the unknown path in preference to the ways of the material world. This is the narrow door and the narrow road that leads to demise of the self-centered ego and the emergence of a new liberated Self—the Presence of Christ-consciousness. We receive Light in our heart when we are capable of such an in-dwelling.

A taste for simplicity, silence, humility, and modesty are parts of the worldview of a contemplative. There is a refusal to play the games of the material society and its aggressive, ambitious, and self-important display. A contemplative chooses not to set as a goal to get ahead in the material world and does not believe in letting themselves be a passive participant in society's conventional values. There is neither contempt for any aspect of society nor any desire to rule or be ruled.

Most of all, a contemplative wishes to seek their own true Self. This is accomplished by seeking a God found alone and not one stereotyped by any group or religion. It is best to give up all earthly images one has of God. To hear the still silent voice of God for oneself is the pearl of great value.

Contemplatives believe one cannot find personal freedom by getting rid of inhibitions and obligations and thus live a self-centered life. This results in the decay of the true Self. A life of ambition, pleasure, and of constant striving for wealth is seen as nothing short of slavery. This form of slavery keeps one living for material things that are always out of reach, creating the duality between the present in which one does not possess what one seeks and the future that holds all man's desire.

Another lovely example of living a contemplative life to be found only in the moment is described in the Chinese philosophy of the *Tao of Wu Wei,* which articulates the non-action or non-doing, which is not intent on results and not concerned with consciously made plans. If one lives in harmony, the answer will make itself known intuitively when the time comes to act. This action will be based upon a connection with the divine source of all good. It is like sticking a knife into a well-baked cake and finding upon withdrawal no cake stuck to the knife (that is, there is no resistance).

Contemplation is a lifestyle and a worldview. As we have been taught to define success in material terms, this way of being rejects such values. The search for Truth is the ultimate expression of life and an esoteric understanding of scripture is necessary to arrive at this Truth. Love of the Divine in all of its expressions is the driving energy behind the search. A detachment from all things selfish frees us from misplacing our energy into devices of this world.

Meditation

"It was at this point that the seers retired
into the forest to meditate. Thus, from being a relatively
external religion, centered on the fire sacrifice, it
became an interior religion. They sought to build the fire in
the heart. The word tapas mean 'asceticism, self-control,
discipline'—there is no exact translation—but its
original meaning was 'heat.' The belief was that when one
practiced this self-discipline, one generated an
inner heat, an inner fire, and so instead of building the fire

outside and making offerings to God on it, one built the
fire within and offered one's thoughts, one's sins,
one's whole being in this interior fire. This is the turning
point: interior religion manifests itself, and all the depth
of Hindu religion stems from that movement."

—*Bede Griffiths*, **The Cosmic Revelation**

So much has been written and taught about meditation that thinking about it is a major hindrance in achieving the silence of the right hemisphere. The best thing to do is to forget everything you ever thought you knew about meditating. Let's start with "I don't know." This silences the mind as there is no attempt to go back into memory to find an answer that is not meditation anyway. With "I don't know," the mind is devoid of all technique and all definitions of meditation. There is an absence of thought that exists in the past and projects into the future. Now the mind is free, sensitive, and silent, abiding in the vast space of the indescribable and infinite presence of God. When the mind is free and sensitive, this is meditation.

Meditation is communion with the God of your understanding. God is the well-spring of joy, harmony, love, and wisdom. The positive states of joy, love, and harmony are present in us at birth. They are our birthright. The spiritual journey is a reclaiming of these states as we reduce the impact of the ego and its anger, hate, prejudice, and sadness in order to discover that which we really are—Christ-consciousness.

Many will give up the practice of meditation because they find it so difficult to quiet their minds. The brain must be trained as it is used to running all over the place like a little monkey and will resist when you first start to pull in the reins. Keep working at it and soon you will find that the moments of silence become more frequent and of greater duration. Don't try to control the mind. Use your sacred word (Centering Prayer), breath, etc., to bring you back to the moment when the mind starts to "chatter." That's really all there is to it. Sit in peace and when the mind and its thoughts interrupt, bring yourself back to the moment.

During these moments of silence, God can come to visit whenever He wishes and whenever the necessity arises. Since God is omnipresent, you do not have to reach out to Him. God is everywhere and in everything. All of what we see and cannot see is an expression of the "Oneness" of God and His creation. Meditation is inviting God into our being to speak with us, to heal us, and to change the way we see the world. Remember where you are, God already is. Relax and come to rest in God. Let go with both hands (a scary proposition for those with control issues), trust in God, and allow Him to minister to you. Let go of all of the sorrows and pain of the past and remember with God all things are possible.

Meditation (especially Centering Prayer) can be viewed as a method of surrender from a psychological point of view. Here we surrender ourselves to a divine therapist and by relaxing the conscious mind, uncover the unconscious. It does not try to reprogram the conscious mind but cleans out the unconscious where all of our egoic conditioning lurks. The false self is dismantled, thus allowing the true Self to emerge. Old unconscious hurts are released from the body, sometimes bringing tears and symptoms of anxiety. For some, the release of the old hurts creates an unbearable situation. When there is a history of early life trauma, a psychotherapist will generally be helpful, if not necessary, in order to work through the trauma and conceptualize its impact on body, mind, and soul.

Meditation can be considered based upon the goal of the practitioner. For example, if one is looking for psychophysiological health benefits, there are formulas one can learn. Here we are measuring where we have been and where we are going with regard to problems such as hypertension. This is a very good thing, as we can receive measured feedback. However, comparison is an egoic pursuit.

My preference is the use of what might be called unfocused meditation. Being aware in the moment is more of a right-hemisphere orientation. When we are aware, we see the forest and miss the tree. I mean "unfocused" in the sense that there is no clear starting point such as concentrating on a mantra. These types of focused practices start in the left hemisphere as language resides there. The left hemisphere sees the tree but misses the forest. Examples of unfocused practices are Centering Prayer from Contemplative Christianity and mindfulness derived from Zen Buddhism.

I examined Centering Prayer in my last book. In the works of Father Thomas Keating, you can find a beautiful approach to Centering Prayer expressed as a form of Divine Therapy. One can find a great amount of information on mindfulness. The works of Jon Kabat-Zinn are research-based and reveal the health, as well as the spiritual, benefits of the practice. Thich Nhat Hanh and many others have written about mindfulness as a spiritual practice.

For those who are looking for the "Truth," there is no formula. There is only the silence and serenity of the nontemporal right hemisphere waiting for however long is necessary for the still silent voice of God. Here we are looking for a spiritual intervention as God is the only one who can remove our defects of character, change our spiritual worldview, and free us from the burdens of this life. There is no sense of measurement of where I have been and where I wish to go. All is turned over to God. To see clearly, the distortions of the ego must be removed, allowing the experience of "Truth."

Alcohol and drugs can, for a brief period of time, make the brain more sensitive by liberating us from the pettiness of our pasts. However, addiction only dulls the mind. If we are using meditation as a means to something—trying to achieve some altered state of consciousness—it is just like a drug. Even the repetition of words in Sanskrit or Latin make the mind dull as language is more of a left hemisphere phenomenon. Using meditation as a way to escape from the ephemeral world is nothing but an escape and gets us no closer to the "Truth."

Anything that is an escape from "what is" is not meditation. To meditate, one needs a free and orderly mind. This mind is not free from something but exists in a state of freedom. This is a sensitive mind capable of spending time in the silence of the moment. It is in the moment that we can encounter the beauty and wonder of the world. From this experience, one understands the perfection of creation.

I believe meditation is not something we perform at odd times such as for an hour in the evening. Like our change in worldview, meditation needs to pervade our daily living in such a way that we can be mindful of the moment. In the moment, we will know what to do and how to do it. Wrestling with the past and projecting events into the future lead to decisions based on old memories. There is nothing new and creative in thoughts coming from the past. Thinking does not lead us to Truth.

Meditation is to perceive—to be aware of—Truth in each moment. It is not about becoming aware of the Truth ultimately. In a world full of noise and other sensations, the five senses take us on a roller-coaster ride in the land of illusion. The ego loves such experiences and compares each new experience to those stored in memory. Meditation is about this beautiful moment full of infinite power where grace might visit us if conditions are right.

Silence and Solitude

"All spiritual traditions value Silence.
The Tao Te Ching speaks of the Tao as 'for lack of a
better word, the Great Way. It flows, circles, flows and circles.
And it has no name.' So described, the Tao is probably
the same as Silence, for the currents of Silence that
I describe in this book are within this kind of imagination.
Meister Eckhart says of Silence: 'The central silence is the
purest element of the soul, the soul's most exalted place,
the core, the essence of the soul.'"

—*Robert Sardello*, Silence the Mystery of Wholeness

Solitude might be thought of as the furnace where transformation takes place. As long as we stay entangled in a society pandering to the illusions of the ego, we will not grow spiritually. As long as Madison Avenue seduces the ego, we will stay far removed from our Self. We can be proud of the fact we are so busy and "always on the go." We can wear greed in our expensive clothing and show it in our luxury cars. But what is the price we pay for these attachments? All pleasure is accompanied by the duality of pain. Pain is not the most significant price we pay—we pay with our souls.

We are all tempted by worldly compulsions. Even Jesus had his temptations. He was tempted to be relevant and "turn stones into loaves of bread." He was tempted to be spectacular and "throw himself down from the roof of the temple." Finally, he was tempted to become powerful in the material world, and, when offered all the kingdoms of this world, he calmly turned them down.

Solitude is where we struggle with the compulsions of the ego and, as we do so, encounter a loving God. Here we are Lord—naked, vulnerable, sinful, weak, and broken. We are nothing, and we know nothing. It is in this state of "nothingness" that we ask God to dismantle all the false beliefs of the ego—all the anger, fear, greed, pride, envy, and jealousy—one piece at a time. This can be a dreadful experience as we observe our pettiness and want desperately to run back to the comfort of work, friends, alcohol, drugs, spending, or food. However, isn't it more dreadful to deal with the angst caused by the great division between the ego and the stirring of Christ-consciousness within? This is the real sin. It is following a material path and not becoming that which we truly are—the Presence of Christ-consciousness inside us.

There is an existential dread found in the doubt and self-questioning, which sooner or later arises when we live the life of the ego. Inside us, we know this is not the way, but it seems so difficult to break the attachments to those things in life that take us away from the realization of the Presence of Christ within. This dread is a feeling of insecurity, a sense of being lost and in exile. As Jackson Browne sang in his song "The Pretender," it is like being trapped between the longing for love (true connection) and the struggle for money (materialism). There is resignation in his struggle as he sells out for the legal tender and the things that money can buy while going through life with dark glasses on, realizing true love could have been a contender. In the song, Browne sings of realizing that there is a greater awakening that love can bring about. He starts out so young and strong but, over time, surrenders to Madison Avenue–hype where ads enslave the heart and soul of the spender. This lovely song defines beautifully the conflict between the ego and the longing for Christ-consciousness. This conflict leads to an existential dread that dark glasses and material objects cannot overcome.

There is the awareness of living a lie, as we are untrue to the urging of our innermost Self. This is the angst, and it can motivate us to move forward in our search. There is an incredible freedom in the honesty of admitting to ourselves, "Yes, I am not being loyal to my true Self, and, yes, I am living the life of a charlatan." To understand with every fiber of your being that, "Yes, I am a pretender" opens you up to the unknown. The humility of this truth is what allows us to pursue a new way of living—to be born again. Now we are teachable.

The failure to meet the challenge of an existential demand in one's life creates the general sense of failure, anxiety, and guilt that hopefully motivates us to change. There is a deep and profound awareness of a basic antagonism between one's earthly existence and God. This antipathy is caused by the estrangement from Him due to a perverse attachment to the ways of the ego. We can choose to change or rush back into our attachments.

Existential dread can be a very positive step on the spiritual path. I can vividly remember an incident in my life from around twenty-five years ago. I was alone for a weekend in a hotel room in Minnesota. The sense of being a fake and a fraud was so profound I started to cry and proceeded to get down on my knees, asking God to please help me. I could not go on living this way. All of the things I prayed to be and wanted to be were incongruent with the way I was actually living my life. I was turned inside out and no longer had to spend inordinate amounts of energy defending my ego. I believe most of us have to go through dread, anguish, trouble, and fear in order for the maturity of the spiritual life to become the most important focus of our lives. It is only in the complete surrender to God that the process of abandoning our ego can take place. With God's Love, the dread is turned into love, confidence, and hope.

These struggles in solitude are very real as we have lived our whole life as one long defense against the reality of "what is"—our true condition. When we confront our "nothingness," we are led to unconditionally surrender ourselves to God. We realize it is not really us that live but the Christ living within us. This is our Self, and all the rest is just illusion as it exists but is not real. This surrendering is far removed from giving up or giving in and is an understanding that the world is just the way God planned for it to be, and, as long as I try to control, judge, and manipulate it, I can never find peace. There is a wonderful paradox in this lesson. The ego believes happiness is found in controlling people, places, and things in order to get "more and better." To find the happiness the ego strives for, it must give up the illusion of control, which for the ego is to give up aspects of itself.

As the ego is weakened, the compulsions expressed as defects of character start to melt away as the Light of the Self starts to shine through. This is the beginning of the freedom that comes as a child of God.

Solitude is really not a means to an end, as it is its own end. Here is where God remodels us in His own image. Part of the makeover is learning how to die to this temporal and materialistic world, including to the people we know. In this death, we give up measuring ourselves and our value by using a grandiose yardstick. To die to our neighbors means to discontinue judging them and accept them as perfectly where they need to be to learn the lessons they are here to learn in this lifetime. It is to realize that no one does anything to you or for you—it is just consciousness flowing, bringing with it the lessons that provide opportunities for our growth. For only when we have given up the need to control, the compulsion to judge, and the continuous comparison leading to envy and jealousy can we truly have compassion for another. Compassion cannot possibly coexist with judgmentalism, and, without judgmentalism, forgiveness becomes possible.

The Twelfth Step of Alcoholics Anonymous reads as follows, "Having had a spiritual awakening as the result of these Steps, we tried to carry this message to alcoholics, and to practice these principles in all our affairs." Carrying the message is called service work. It should be provided with unconditional love without any motive or expectation of anything in return from the other. Here one receives joy and peace, which is a foreign language to the ego. I believe you get the point. Until I can rid myself, to a significant degree, of the defects of character, I cannot give love for love's sake and cannot receive the blessings of "peace and joy."

One of the definitions of yoga is "skill in action" or "wisdom in work." In this way, one is in perfect harmony with all of God's creation and can act spontaneously or freely. Like the *Tao of Wu Wei*, it is based on faith in the moment and awareness that right action and right thought will occur as needed. Whenever we perform any kind of work, it should be done for the love of the work. There should be no seeking of personal reward, as the fruits of our labors should be left as a sacrifice to God. If the ego enters the work, we will feel personal gratification if it is successful and depressed if it fails. It becomes personalized as "I'm no good."

As an individualized culture, Americans tend to be egoic in all matters. When everything flows through us, it puts a lot of pressure on the "I" and "me" to continually produce so we might be able to say (unless we are perfectionistic and self-critical) to ourselves, "I am good" and "I am successful." This grandiose worldview creates a steady level of stress and misery. So short-term, one can feel angry, anxious, fearful, or depressed and in the longer term suffer from stress-related diseases such as coronary disease, cancer, obesity, hypertension, etc.

Contemplation, meditation, silence and solitude, and prayer are methods that reduce the stress of life by putting us in harmony with God's creation. The time and dedication required to learn and perfect these methods yield great benefits in terms of managing functional day-to-day stress and in the greater achievement of a harmonious existence. Harmony is an inner light of wisdom guiding your actions in the moment. Another term for "harmony" is *complete faith* in God's ability to guide our life. Think of a wild animal like the mongoose. A mongoose can kill a cobra, but it must know exactly when to attack and not allow the snake to strike first. The mongoose is not guided by ego but by its connection to the rhythm and flow of nature. If it had to think about all of the possibilities and doubts, the snake would probably put an end to its life.

When we are not at peace with ourselves, being in silence and solitude can be very uncomfortable. We are trying to discover more of, and spend more time in, the nonlinear spiritual realm. It is quite a new experience for many people. Often new experiences are uncomfortable. Historically, we have found comfort in putting to words an experience as this seems to give us a sense of control—a grasp of the experience so to speak. There is no language for the subjective and the spiritual. Therefore, "Truth" and the "Actual" cannot be expressed in words. When we experience the intuitive, the "ah ha" experience, as Truth and try to put words to the experience it is no longer Truth. Silence and solitude take us outside our comfort zone of words and reason. Reason, no matter how unreasonable gives the ego the false sense of being in control.

Silence is the first language of God. There is no greater form of intelligence than silence. Silence completes and intensifies solitude. The Word of God is born out of the eternal silence of the Godhead. This is the still silent voice one becomes aware of during meditation. All the words of the material dualistic world cannot equal what one intuits from the still and silent voice. Coordinate yourself with the greater being found in silence.

We can say silence is the mystery of the future world beyond this life. In this way, silence makes us pilgrims as we leave the comfort of our vocabulary and worldly affairs and journey into the unknown world of the mystery. As our words are often an expression of our doubts and not our faith, silence as mother gives birth to our wisest and most profound thoughts. If we need to use words, those coming from the power of Christ-consciousness will bear fruit. Those spoken from the controlling ego will cause us and others misery and suffering. Power (unconditional love) always overcomes control (force).

But let your words be yes, yes and no, no;
for anything which adds to these is deception.

—MATTHEW 5:37

Become a lover of silence and escape from the noisy milieu. In solitude, we abscond from the busy world. Solitude and silence are for prayer. Remember the following:

Solitude is not being alone, it is being with God.
Silence is not total silence, it is listening to God.
Solitude and silence are the context within
which prayers are practiced.

Prayer

But you when you pray, enter into your inner chamber,
And pray to your Father who is in secret,
And your Father who sees in secret He Himself
Shall reward you openly.

—*MATTHEW 6:6*

By entering into our inner chamber, we are choosing to close the door on the outside world. Here we can let go of the everyday problems in order to spend time with God. In our inner chamber, we shut down the "chatter" of the mind and move into our heart. The heart has four chambers and has a brain of its own. It is a seat of consciousness and its energy field communicates with the greater consciousness of the universe. In the stillness of prayer, in secret, our Self is in communication with God. The reward for prayer in secret is a deeper knowledge of God, which will lead us to live in the Presence of Christ-consciousness.

There is no right or wrong way to pray as long as it is performed from the heart with sincerity. It is important to remember that God is infinite wisdom and infinite love and not a concierge service. Asking for a new car or a million dollars is unlikely to draw a response. I suspect what you ask for and what you get are more related to "needs," as opposed to "wants."

There is a trick phrase in the Lord's Prayer. It doesn't say "my will be done" but "*thy will be done.*" Prayer is a turning over of our will to God and being open to His will working through us. You might ask for humility and end up being a narcissistic alcoholic and addict. What a wonderful spiritual opportunity, as humility is a necessary spiritual tool to deflate the grandiose pride of the ego.

I believe the best prayer is silence. One might ask for the courage and strength to perform God's will or even to have God's will revealed to us. These revelations or intuitive experiences happen when the mind is silent. The first language of God is silence—the silence behind everything, including all the noise of nature and noise made by all of the people and machinery of the world. For some, silence is what exists between various noises. For others, this silence always exists and has depth. If in our prayerful state we can approximate this deep silence, we are speaking the same language as God. Here we might be able to hear the still silent voice of God as an impartation of Truth.

A translation for the words *pray always* is "come to rest." The Greek word for "rest" is *hesychia*. A hesychast is one who seeks solitude and silence as ways to unceasing prayer. "Come to rest" is a respite in God in the midst of intense daily activity. When life gets overwhelming, the silence is always there. There is no conflict in the silence—only the peace of God.

In the Old Testament, the only name we have for God is the Hebrew YHWH, a "word," so to speak, never intended to be pronounced. This "word" seems to translate into "I Am." The spiritual aspirant then approaches God in silence and in silence is rewarded.

The further along the spiritual path one is, the more one learns to let God do the praying for him. Here the Presence of Christ-consciousness prays for you, bears witness for you, and makes intercession for you. God knows what you need, so there is little need in asking Him. He is the only one who understands your needs both for today as well as for tomorrow. Joel Goldsmith describes this beautifully in *The Heart of Mysticism* when he writes, "You come to a very high state of spiritual illumination as you realize that you do not know how to pray, and that all you can do is to learn to listen and let the Father reveal Himself within you. All power is in God, so let us be receptive and responsive to that Power and Presence of God, and It will do all things through us—even pray! It will not answer our prayers; It will not fulfill our desires; but It will fulfill Its own desires in us!"

In the New Testament, the Book of John Chapter 17 is known as the high priestly prayer. This is a long monologue by Jesus as he speaks to the Father about those given to him—the disciples. Jesus states in verses 15 and 16, "What I request is not that you should take them from the world, but that you should protect them from evil. For they are not of the world, just as I am not of the world." Jesus also requests that the disciples be perfected in "One" asking in verse 21, "So that they all may be one; just as you, my father, art with me, and I am with you, that they also may be one with us; so that the world may believe you sent me."

In this prayer, Jesus is asking for two things for his disciples. The first is that they remain protected from evil, and the second is that they achieve the realization of Christ or God-consciousness, allowing them to be "One" with the Father just as Jesus is "One" with his Father. These two things might be good guidelines for prayer. First, ask God to protect you from the evil elements on earth—the evil in the egos of men and women—and second, ask Him for guidance as you work spiritually toward the realization of Christ-consciousness. Surrounded by silence, this short prayer focuses in on the most important aspect of this life—to become that which we are, our true Self, the Christ within us.

In the New Testament, Jesus Christ tells us the two most important behaviors are to love thy neighbor as thyself and to love God with all of your soul, might, heart, strength, and mind. When we truly follow these commandments and are focused on spiritual evolution, it is highly unlikely one would think about stealing, killing, bearing false witness, or committing adultery. So prayer is to help us stay on the narrow road of the spiritual path and not be seduced by the evil perdition in this world.

In Matthew 5:39, Jesus made a statement that many have a difficult time with. He says, "But I say to you, that you should not resist evil; but whoever strikes you on your right cheek, turn to him the other also." From the perspective of a militarized country such as the United States, the "turn the other cheek" attitude and behavior is overlooked. As I do not write about political topics, I will address this from what I believe Jesus might have had in mind when he proffered this declaration. When we resist evil, evil wins. By resisting, we have justified the actions of the wicked and, in doing so, brought ourselves to the same level of evil. As we have stated previously, power (love) will always, in the long run, overcome force (ego).

God is Love, and who could ask for more than that? He is also omnipotent and omnipresent. God is infinite intelligence. Can we teach God anything He doesn't already know? Do we expect to change perfection? Gratitude is the appropriate response. Not just the verbal expression of gratitude but gratitude in action. Don't you think God would appreciate gratitude as expressed in patience, love, good deeds, and meekness?

Vocal prayer can never do the spiritual work of good deeds. If one believes prayer cancels all wrongdoings, he grows more corrupt by continuing to sin. The belief that all we need to do is ask for pardon and then we can go out and continue to do the same wrong thing compounds the sin. I remember when I was growing up, on Sunday the family always went to church. In the church were carpenters, lawyers, housewives, doctors, truck drivers, etc. All were praying for forgiveness of sin and for salvation. However, Monday through Saturday it was back to the "real" world of "dog eat dog," "hate the communists," and "there is a sucker born every minute." If I don't screw them then someone else will. There were always rationalizations to make sin reasonable.

According to Mary Baker Eddy in her book *Science and Health with Key to the Scriptures*, the test of all prayer lies in the answer to the following questions: "Do we pursue the old selfishness, satisfied with having prayed for something better, though we give no evidence of the sincerity of our requests by living consistently with our prayer? Do we love our neighbor better because of this asking? If selfishness has given place to kindness, we shall regard our neighbor unselfishly, and bless them that curse us; but we shall never meet this great duty simply by asking that it may be done."

Also, do not fear for the future. Be concerned for the present and what we need to do to seek the Kingdom of God. If we are seeking first the Kingdom of God to the best of our abilities, everything we need will be given to us. Like the ninety-first Psalm, the following verses from Matthew tell us that not everyone will be provided for. Only the ones who keep God in their heart working toward Christ-consciousness will fall under the protection of the Lord.

*Therefore do not worry or say, What will we eat, or what
will we drink, or with what will we be clothed?
For worldly people seek after all these things.
Your Father in heaven knows that all of these things
are also necessary for you.*

But you seek first the kingdom of God and His righteousness,
And all of these things shall be added to you.
Therefore do not worry for tomorrow;
For tomorrow will look after its own.
Sufficient for each day, is its own trouble.

—MATTHEW 6:31–34

Seek first the Kingdom of God, and everything you require will be added to you.

Summary

Contemplation, meditation, silence and solitude, and prayer have great similarities in that all seek to move us toward a greater understanding of our true nature and our relationship with God. When we start to combine these practices, the result is usually greater than the sum of the components. This is the crucible where the still silent voice of God can rearrange our lives and change our view of the world.

These changes can occur when the mind is orderly. An orderly mind gets us away from the constant motives of reward and punishment. This kind of mind is not seeking anything and is not capable of illusion as it is the ego that invents experiences it calls insights. These supposed "insights" are nothing more than a reconfiguration of old experiences into something believed by the ego to be new and exciting.

In this chapter, I have used the word "detachment" and discussed being detached on several occasions. The sannyasi renounces all property, but the real renunciation is the renunciation of "I," "me," and "mine." The sannyasi is one who is totally detached from the world and from himself. This is not being unattached. To be totally unattached to the world leads to noninvolvement. Detachment is being in the world but not of it. With detachment there is still the love of service work and a deep caring for the world but a denial of the values of the material world where he who gets the most toys before he dies wins. In actuality, he who gets the most baubles before he dies is just dead.

The issue is not material possessions. You can have a nice car, a fine home, and money in the bank as long as you are not attached to them. When we give energy to material things that should go toward our own spiritual being and important relationships, the material things are an attachment. Giving this energy inappropriately to alcohol, drugs, food, gambling, sex, etc., is an attachment called addiction. When you realize that you can lose all the worldly possessions and addictions and still be alright because you know God will provide for you, detachment becomes possible.

You have to be ready to give up everything—children, parents, wife, husband, property, and home. This is a hard saying. But, most of all, you have to be willing to give up your ego and all of its defects of character. This is the poverty spoken of by Jesus in the Sermon on the Mount. This poverty of spirit is a total detachment from the material world. We must realize everything comes from God and not from

Amazon, Wal-Mart, and Best Buy. We really cannot possess anything. We can, however, receive everything, but only in the moment.

This world has become profane. It has separated God from our daily life. When you are detached from the world, everything becomes a symbol of God. It is only when we become free from self (ego)—our grandiose self-love and self-will—that we can truly love our neighbor and serve the world.

It is during these times of deep meditation and contemplation in a prayerful state of silence and solitude that the still silent voice of God can teach us. It is during this state of reverie that Divine Therapy can take place. Since everything is energy, all of the sorrows, pain, suffering, and misery in our lives are stored in our body and brain in the form of energy. By totally surrendering ourselves to the power of God and asking God to free us from these hurts, energy can be released from our being. This can bring on tears, negative feelings, and a sense of release as this stored energy is freed from the body.

This stored energy most often comes from the conditioning that occurred during early life. These misplaced values are unconscious and impossible to live up to. For example, we will be speaking of Jesus's admonition to be perfect like our Father in heaven. If we are self-critical (we could add any of the defects of character here), we live in a setup for true misery (see *The Ego-Less SELF: Achieving Peace and Tranquility Beyond All Understanding* for further explanation). It often takes a later life crisis to create the pain necessary to get us to seek help.

This release of energy starts to move us toward that which we really are—our true Self. In your inner room, God can start the healing process. Sometimes the hurts are so severe a person needs guidance and support from someone such as a therapist, spiritualist, or psychologist. God is certainly powerful enough to totally rearrange our internal being. However, sometimes we do not believe we are strong enough on our own to manage the resulting freedom. Professional help and self-help can assist us to manage the transition.

Father Thomas Keating puts this process into perspective when he states in *Manifesting God*, "We may be scared of being who we are. Jesus addresses this situation in these words: 'If you try to save your life (that is your false self), you will bring yourself to ruin.' The false self has no future. The second half of the saying is, 'One who brings himself to naught for me discovers who he is' (Matthew 10:39). The true Self is limitless in its spiritual capacity. To bring oneself to nothing, that is, to no particular thing, is to let go of the over-identification with one's body, feelings, thoughts, and one's inmost self, as well as, friends, relatives, property and roles. It also means moderating our exaggerated desires for gratification of our emotional programs for happiness."

We have come to a jumping off point. Through prayer and meditation, we have prepared ourselves and have truly started our spiritual journey. The last chapters of this book will try to look at the term *realization*. We are all perfect and the only difference between any of us is the amount of realized Christ-Consciousness within us. How can one develop a greater realization of the Divine?

Realization can be thought of as the accumulation of more Light. As we gather more Light unto ourselves, our worldview changes. As we see the world differently, our thoughts, feelings, and behaviors toward the world change. We become more detached and start to understand that life is an opportunity for spiritual growth. God isn't trying to be mean or vindictive. Remember God is Love, unlimited wisdom, and everything in this world is an extension of Him. There is nothing that is not sacred.

How can realization be understood? We are entering an area that is difficult to put into words, and words will fail to capture the energy and profound beauty of the realization of Christ-consciousness. When the world becomes beautiful and one can see the love inside everyone and everything, the happiness and joy of our early childhood returns. Now we can appreciate that everything is God, and there is nothing else. Everything is good because good is all God created. Evil is in the minds of men and women and is an illusion called the ego. Remember, in the spiritual world, the only reality is that which has always been here and always will be here. The human ego exists, but it is not real.

The next part looks more closely at realization. I believe we are here to discover our true Self . . . to come to the realization of the Presence of the Christ inside all of us. The term *sin* is a necessary part of this discussion.

Many, if not most, think of sin from the perspective of breaking laws, actions, and deeds. The karmic law of an "eye for an eye" or a "tooth for a tooth" is an Old Testament perspective. As stated previously, in the New Testament, there are two great laws. Love God with all your might and soul and spirit and love your neighbor as yourself. Viewing sin as purely aberrant behavior doesn't give a proper perspective to the spiritual aspirant. Here we are dealing with the symptoms of a lack of self-awareness (that is, Truth). If someone understands the Truth, they would not steal, kill, or take the Lord's name in vain as these are the bad fruit of the desires of the ego.

From a spiritual perspective, sin is a refusal to grow. It is a lack of understanding of our mission through lifetimes. This mission is to realize the presence of Christ-consciousness in ourselves and to seek to become as much like the Christ—the archetype of the perfect man—as we possibly can in this lifetime. To do this, we have to step out of the ordinary. This search takes great commitment and willingness to go against the values of the material world. The model used in the next part is the teachings of Jesus Christ as exemplified in the beatitudes in the Sermon on the Mount.

Jesus tells us to be perfect just as the Father in Heaven is perfect. This is an ultimatum directed to all of us. Jesus Christ achieved perfection, thereby demonstrating the possibility for all men and women. We cannot accomplish Christ-consciousness by believing Jesus became the Christ but by our coming to believe in ourselves what Jesus believed in himself. This is Jesus's message to us—the Truth of the Divinity of man.

Part Three

Realization and Illumination

Chapter Six

Realization

This chapter is about realizing the Christ-consciousness in us. This is our "Oneness" with God. We have looked at the crucible. Now it is time to look at increasing our contact with God and allowing more Light into ourselves. We will be embarking on a long and narrow road leading to perfection or total realization of Christ-consciousness. Creation involves the evolution of man and the creations of the abilities to not only ask the important question but to be able to discern the answers. This is a story of millions upon millions of years of neural development.

Over time, as the prefrontal cortex developed, men and women became able to think beyond themselves and their basic needs. Thinking beyond simple survival needs, our ancestors naturally began to wonder about the "whys" of life. Phenomenon such as lightning and the discovery of fire led to the development of various superhuman spiritual entities or gods. The ancient priests, shamans, and mystics were revered because of their supposed ability to commune with this spiritual world.

From prehistoric times, our ancestors had the idea that this physical life on earth was not the ending point. There was something more. There was the belief that man came into this world from a spiritual form. When physical life was terminated, the soul left this earth and returned to a spiritual realm.

Over time, man's search for the mystical became internalized as he realized his Creator was immanent and lived inside himself. The Hindu culture speaks of Shiva Nataraja, the Dancing Shiva, as a part of the cosmic revelation. In *The Cosmic Revelation*, Bede Griffiths states, "He is one of the great figures in Indian mythology. He is represented with four arms dancing in a circle of fire, dancing at the heart of creation. It is a cosmic dance: it represents the power which permeates the whole universe. The idea is that God is dancing in the heart of creation and in every human heart. We must find the Lord who is dancing in our hearts; then we will see the Lord dancing in all of creation."

In a crucial period of human history that started in the middle of the first millennium before Christ, breakthroughs were made, allowing man to move toward an intimate experience of the ultimate reality. This reality that transcends all words is called Brahman and Atman (the Spirit) in Hinduism, Tao (the Way) in China, Being in Greece, Yahweh ("I am") in Judaism, and Nirvana and Sunyata (the Void) in

Buddhism. These are mere words attempting to conceptualize the ultimate meaning of life, which no human thought can express.

In the Christian faith, the Godhead is the unspoken mystery. We use words such as *Trinity* to describe the indescribable. The *Father, Son,* and the *Holy Spirit* are viewed as three entities in one being. They are nonlinear as the manifestations of the Godhead. As Bede Griffiths beautifully states in *Return to Center*, "To understand the mystery of the Trinity it is necessary to participate in the experience of Jesus. It is necessary to receive the Spirit of God, to share in the divine life and so to become the son of God, to be one with Jesus as he is one with the Father (John 17:11). This is the mystery of Christianity, the participation in the inner life of the Godhead, a mystery which cannot be expressed in words, but which is indicated by analogy by the words 'Father', 'Son' and 'Spirit'. If we stop at the words or the concepts signified by them, we shall always remain outside, unenlightened. But if we pass beyond the words and the concepts to the reality signified by them, then we know the Truth, then we are one with God."

Built into our human makeup is the thirst for wholeness—to connect with our Creator. This quest leads one to the most important questions of life such as, "What do I believe and what is my relationship to this belief?" Based upon our beliefs, certain other questions arise such as, "Would I rather stay on the old road of life or am I willing to do what it takes to advance spiritually?" We know what the same old road leads to. Where can the new, narrower road guide us?

The same old road is living life as we know it.... It is linear, temporal, conditioned, controlling, and constantly striving to become some image or illusion. It leads to searching for happiness outside ourselves, feeling "worn out," and craving new experiences. It is the same routine, boring, and unfulfilling way of being in this materialistic world. It is trying to live life as we believe it "should be" or "could be."

So what is the alternative? What is the new narrower road leading to Christ-consciousness? This road is nonlinear, inward, attained by removing images and illusions, silent, and in the moment. There is neither a map to the destination nor any comfort zone or attachments to fall back into. It is high-wire act without a net. This is one of the reasons such care should be taken in one's search when considering teachers and writings. Spiritual deception is the greatest deception of all.

This road leads back to the feeling of life and is always vibrant. Here is where beauty, unconditional love, and the Truth reside. This is the road to the realization of Christ-consciousness. If we had the choice, most would choose the new road. Unfortunately, not very many are willing to put in the effort as "We just don't have the time."

There is also little or no immediate gratification to constantly incentivize us. When you can get a six to seven second "mental orgasm" from taking a hit off a crack pipe or in thirty minutes find relief in a pill, a life of dedication and devotion living for your Creator and not for your ego doesn't look very appealing.

The same old way is living life for the next flashy and trendy thing, the next thrill. But when we finally realize we are living for the God of our understanding and not for our ego, the practices of meditation, contemplation, silence and solitude, and prayer start to make sense.

As we see this life as an opportunity to move closer to the realization of our Source, living a humble life becomes beautiful.

The old and new roads are diametrically opposite each other. When we live by the new road, we will look different from those on the old road. Jesus Christ tells us we have to leave our families and friends and old ways of being in order to follow the new road.

Table 4. Old Road Versus New Road

SAME OLD ROAD (Linear)	LEADS TO
Temporal	Searching for happiness outside of self
Conditioned	Feeling "worn out"
Acquiring	Still craving experiences
Becoming	Unfulfilled
Images	What "should" be
Illusions	Can be routine and boring
Concentration	
Controlling	
"Chattering" mind	

NEW ROAD (Linear)	LEADS TO
Being and awareness	"The feeling"
No map	Heart becomes involved
In the moment	Unconditional love

NEW ROAD (Linear)	LEADS TO
Silence	Beauty
Attained by removing	Meditation
Images and illusions	"What is"
Action not thought	Truth
Awareness	Always new
	"Wu wei"

Table 4: This table contrasts the differences between living life as one has always lived it and how life can be if lived from the heart and in a spiritual way. Life becomes an old conditioned way of seeing, thinking about, and doing things. There is little free will while traveling the "old road." One is living by the conditioning that developed the ego. The new road can be very difficult as one has to look at one's self in the light of who one really is instead of living behind the mask of the ego. The question is, "Which way will you choose?" There is no middle ground. You are either the Light or you are living in darkness.

There are many who try to stand in the middle of the road. They know enough about their religious beliefs to speak eloquently but not enough to give real and lasting joy, peace, happiness, and abundance in life. These individuals refuse to regard themselves as of this material world but do not truly enter into the spiritual life. Deep inside they know they are charlatans, and they will soon be found out as they are spiritual egotists.

This new road leads ultimately to Christ-consciousness. Its reservoir of unlimited power cannot be used for selfish purposes. Maybe this is also a reason why the world lacks interest in developing this level of conscious realization. It is not about "What's in it for me?" but it is about loving your neighbor as yourself. Giving of yourself and not getting something for ego gratification defines the code of conduct. Realization starts with emptying ourselves so we can receive grace.

All of the things necessary for our well-being will be supplied to us in abundance once we give up the effort and desire for them and wish only to fulfill our destiny here on earth. All of us are a part of a Divine plan. We are consciousness expressing itself. Therefore, forget yourself and live in a state of receptivity to the Christ-consciousness inside you. The desire of living for the ego will be a stumbling block in spiritual development. Desire comes from a sense of not being complete. We are all complete; we just have to realize the fact.

Our degree of spiritual consciousness can be measured to the extent we have given up the material world and placed our faith in something greater then ourselves. In John 14:27, Jesus said, "Peace I leave with you; my own peace I give you; not as the world gives you, I give to you. Let not your heart be troubled, and do not be afraid." Here Jesus is telling us we will not find peace if we look to the world to attain it. "My peace" has nothing to do with this world but is a peace within that nothing outside can disrupt.

One of the things I discovered over the years is that peace is a much more desirable state than happiness. I always thought it was happiness I wanted. To be happy, one must experience the duality of unhappiness. There are by relationship the ups and downs of this life. Peace just flows like a stream . . . always there with very few ripples.

Peace comes when the ego and its need to live up to some false set of standards is removed.

We are deliberating about living in harmony with consciousness. In *Practicing the Presence*, Joel Goldsmith states, "The degree of spiritual consciousness which we attain can be measured by the extent to which we relinquish our dependence on the external world of form and place our faith and confidence in something greater than ourselves, in the Infinite Invisible, which can surmount any and every obstacle. It is awareness of the grace of God." The Truth realized is spiritual consciousness. This Truth comes from our receptivity born of the practices of meditation, contemplation, silence and solitude, and prayer. God is available to us only in proportion to our degree of realization and willingness to devote ourselves to the attainment of the perfection of Jesus Christ.

We know the Spirit has entered when we start letting go of anger, hatred, prejudice, jealousy, envy, and other defects of character. We know when our worldview changes such that we see more love and beauty in God's perfect world.

Many believe they will have peace if they just have enough of everything they need—money, relationships, material goods—to be secure. Since security is an illusion (one cannot predict the future), this approach obviously will not work. As long as we look to people, places, things, and situations for peace, we will not find it. It is complete reliance on our Creator that brings the visible into our awareness as we have a need for it. The question is, "What do you rely on?" Do you put your faith in the form or what created the form? Like the sannyasi, do you worship the sign or what signifies it?

Douleuein is the Greek word meaning "to serve" or "to be given over to." In Latin the word *addicere* (addiction) is similar and means "to be given over to" or "under the control of" a force outside oneself. By determining what we are "given over to," we can predict what is controlling a person's life. In other words, we can tell what preoccupies their heart.

The world we see, taste, hear, smell, and touch is the world Jesus overcame. "These things I have said to you, that in me you may have peace. In the world you will have tribulation; but have courage; I have conquered the world," said Jesus in John 16:33. This world our senses perceive is not the real world. What is real is invisible and cannot be sought. What we believe to be real is a world formed by our senses. The world of the senses is not under the law of God. However, this world is under the grace of God, and we must choose to realize this grace. This is the realization of Christ-consciousness within us.

In the world of the senses, there is always an opposite. There is light and dark, rough and smooth, sweet and sour, good and bad, good fortune and bad fortune, winning and losing, and so on. Life thus becomes an effort to change one of the pairs of opposites into the other. For example, if I am poor I strive to be rich, and, if I don't believe I am beautiful, I strive to make myself beautiful. Understand that the Kingdom of God is a spiritual universe where there are no qualities and quantities. The Kingdom of God is about the realization of spiritual truths and has nothing to do with worldly, materialistic effects.

There are many approaches to realization. Each culture has its own beliefs and spiritual methodologies. I believe all are to be valued. The established methods such as Judaism, Buddhism, Islam, Hinduism, Native practices, and Christianity have a long history of leading disciples to enlightenment if followed diligently. These I believe to be the most valuable of all ways. As you know, the approach I take in this book is contemplative Christian based upon the Sermon on the Mount and in particular the beatitudes. Here Jesus the Christ gives us a way to strive for perfection. For many, this is an immediate turnoff as "No one can be perfect." But, in fact, this is what achieving Christ-consciousness is all about. As we progress through the trials and tribulations of lifetimes, gaining a greater understanding as we go, our task is to work toward the archetype of the Christ—the perfect man or woman. Yes, it is difficult. It goes against all of the values of the material world. Don't beat yourself up over this; just use it as a way to see where you are going. To accomplish this to the best of your understanding is not impossible. This is what Jesus taught, and I believe he expects us to live this way. Don't look outside yourself, for the Kingdom of God is within you if you are a true believer. Perfection may occur as we pass from this life into the next. As I have stated, I believe it takes many lifetimes to work through all of the problems and achieve the realization of Christ-consciousness. I could be wrong as I really don't know anything other than the "knowingness" of walking down the narrow road.

Depending upon where you are in your spiritual development, in some people the characteristics of the beatitudes are better developed than others. This is because some of us have more ego to overcome than others. One might say the spirit of one individual has had more lifetimes to reduce the impact of the ego and to gain Light. At the end, everyone will achieve this level of perfection. Since none of the descriptions of perfection speak to the natural egoic disposition, we are dependent upon grace alone to provide for us. However, we have to diligently persevere in order to do our part. This is where meditation, contemplation, silence and solitude, and prayer come in. This is also where our spiritual study and overt behavior show our shift in character. Our ambition should be different from the masses. You will notice in yourself a rustling and dissonance when you perceive that the things that used to seem so natural and right no longer are working for you in this world.

In Matthew 5:13, we are told we are "the salt of the earth." This tells us something about what we must do with our lives. Although we are in this world but not of it, each of us has to do our part to positively impact this world. Governments, policies, treaties, and summits will never make a difference in this world. There is no mandate that causes humans to change internally, and that is what the world needs. We are singled out as individuals, and, as such, we are the only thing that can save this world full of deceit and pollution.

The world is becoming more foul and offensive with time. Salt is the treatment used to prevent the development of a putrid state. Think of how it is used on meat to kill bacteria and to prevent decay as a preservative. So we are to be like salt in the world. Just by being a spiritual person, your character, disposition, and ways of being in the world control the space you abide in. Your high level of spiritual energy emanates forth from you and influences your immediate environment.

You may notice people with problems come to you for guidance. Without your saying a word, they solve their problem. It is your spiritual energy entraining them that allows for solution. Another can utilize your energy (Light is information) when within your energy field. You change the energy field around you and bring positive spiritual energy into the world. Imagine what millions upon millions of spiritually advanced individuals would do to change the course of civilization. This is the only way cultures will change, and the world becomes a better place.

When you approach a group of people gossiping and/or acting in crude ways, do you notice how they change because of your presence? You do not have to even say a word. Your spiritual energy is what changes things. You are to be unlike the majority of people in the world. The beatitudes tell us how we are to live in order to change ourselves and this world while preparing for the mystery to come.

Do not look at the beatitudes as a code of ethics or morals but as a description of character. It is not a new Ten Commandments but rather a description of what a Christian is meant to be. As D. Martyn Lloyd-Jones states in *Studies in the Sermon on the Mount,* "If you find yourself arguing with the Sermon on the Mount at any point, it means either there is something wrong with you or else that your interpretation of the Sermon is wrong. I find that very valuable."

Let us all examine ourselves carefully. As we study the beatitudes, we may well feel a sense of unworthiness. I continue to mourn because of the comparison to the perfection of Jesus Christ. I fall so short of the ideal. But if it is our desire and ambition to strive to be like Jesus, the Kingdom is within and we are citizens.

The beatitudes will make it clear as to how we are to be in this world. It is interested in our character before our conduct. If you have right character, you will behave accordingly. It is the path to true happiness, and like salt it adds savor to our lives. There is little need for the outside thrills and experiences of the world because, when you are internally at peace in your heart, nothing else is necessary. As I have written several times, the external forms of happiness are fleeting and always will bring displeasure. So set your sites on something more fulfilling and more enduring, and do not evaluate your worth based upon worldly measures such as wealth and numbers of possessions. You are not alright just because you have the right car and wear the right clothes. The only approval that matters is in the eyes of God.

The beatitudes ask us to grow up into our spiritual Self and to leave the ego behind. Understand peace is found by emptying one's self and becoming Selfless—egoless. Jesus is the embodiment of the beatitudes. He lived them and taught them. He was and still is the Light of the world.

When Jesus told those assembled, "You are the light of the world," he was speaking to the poor, the sick, the workers, and those without great material means. He wasn't talking to a summit full of religious or political leaders but *to you and to me.*

We understand much of this world is in a state of darkness, but yet we often hear the term *enlightened.* This term *enlightened* has become a favorite phrase since the Renaissance of the fifteenth and sixteenth century. In the eighteenth century, the term *Enlightenment* was used to define the era. What was the term used to describe? It was based upon the amount of new knowledge being gained and was the beginning of what is generally described as modern civilization. This knowledge was mostly in the area of science.

The important question to ask is "Does this knowledge solve the problems of mankind?" The answer is a resounding no! Science and its understanding of nature and disease have given us an incredible amount of extremely valuable tools. Because of it, we live longer and materially better lives. However, when we look at the darkness of the world, has this knowledge alleviated the basic problems of our planet? Hate, prejudice, and poverty still abound. In the Garden of Eden, how can so many be so hungry? Poverty is an indication that God's plan is not being fulfilled and is a call to all of us to be of service.

An incredible number of schemes have been invented to bring about happiness in the world. They all endeavor to make changes to external situations while leaving the inside of man totally unchanged. The results have always been the same—complete and utter failure. It is only by changing the consciousness of man that outer conditions can be altered. Science cannot do this.

One must follow the narrow road while resisting the magnetism of the material world and the impact of subliminal marketing on the thrill-seeking ego. Maybe the biggest problem is the belief that we are "only human." We are divine in our creation and limitless in our potential. We must understand that Newtonian physics explains the limited or material world but does not in any way explain the unlimited world of the spirit.

This reminds me of Friedrich Nietzsche's *Parable of the Madman*, in which a madman is running through the streets seeking God and saying to onlookers that we have killed Him (God is dead). I believe Nietzsche was saying that because science will solve all of the world's problems there will be no need for God. The mystery will be discovered. Well this is not the case and never will be. Arguably, the world is getting worse and not better.

Part of the problem is we are primarily interested in scientific, biological, and mechanical knowledge. Our knowledge of the real meaning of life has not increased at all. The character and deportment of the citizens of this world reflect a lack of understanding of spiritual wisdom. We have lost the reason for our existence.

If we are to be the Light of the world, we do not need more scientific knowledge but require genuine spiritual understanding. Each spiritual approach tells us how to translate philosophy (worldview) into action. Unfortunately, the true spiritual masters and their teachings are habitually ignored. So what are you and I as spiritual activists supposed to do?

Jesus promised those that follow Him would not walk in darkness but shall have the Light of life. Not only will we have this Light and be made of it, but we will also become beacons of Light. We will transmit Light into the darkness of the world.

In *Studies on the Sermon of the Mount*, Martyn Lloyd-Jones speaks of how all of this works in the world when he wrote, "In other words Scripture, in dealing with Christians, always emphasizes first what he is, before it begins to speak of what he does. As a Christian, I should always have this general effect upon men before I have this specific effect. Wherever I may find myself, immediately that 'something different' about me should have its effect; and that in turn ought to lead men and women to look at me and say, 'There is something unusual about that man.' Then as they watch my conduct and behavior, they begin to ask me questions. Here, the element of 'light' comes out; I am able to speak and to teach them. Far too often we Christians tend to reverse the order. We have spoken in a very enlightened manner, but we have not always lived as the salt of the earth. Whether we like it or not, our lives should always be the first thing to speak and if our lips speak more than our lives it will avail very little. So often the tragedy has been that people proclaim the gospel in words, but their whole life and demeanor has been a denial of it. The world does not pay much attention to them."

Light exposes the darkness and all the hidden things that are a part of it. Light also explains the darkness. The cause of darkness in the world is the estrangement from our spiritual being. The world rewards the profanity of the ego—its selfishness and self-promotion. The world looks up to people who establish their riches by ripping off others. Even the most heinous criminals have their followings. The world desires darkness more than it desires the Light. Although one knows what is right, there is a preference for darkness. The ego justifies this with rationalizations. Of course, "Everyone is doing it, so why not me!" Of course, "If I ever get as bad as Joe, I'll certainly change." Besides, "What is wrong with having a little fun?"

When people who are pure of heart speak, those of the darkness persecute them. This is because being in the presence of a spiritual person makes them feel so guilty and uncomfortable. Hopefully, these negative feelings will one day or one lifetime lead to an existential dread, piloting one to totally evaluate one's life and the way one is living it.

Ultimately, the answer is to be born again as a child of the Light. "To be born again" means to change one's worldview—to change from the egoic ways that love the darkness to someone who moves in Light. As we review the beatitudes, we grow to understand what walking in the Light really means. We also grow to understand what true riches are. It is not the rewards of this world we are after but something far greater.

For if man thinks himself to be something,
When he is nothing, he deceives himself.
But let every man examine his own work,
And then may he glory within himself alone,
And not among others.
For every man shall bear his own burden.
Let him who is taught the word,
Become a partaker with him who teaches all good things.
Do not be deceived; God is not deceived:
For whatsoever a man sows, that shall he also reap.

He who sows things of the flesh,
from the flesh shall reap corruption;
He who sows things of the Spirit shall reap life everlasting.

—GALATIANS 6:3–8

It is my hope your experience in reading about the beatitudes in the following pages creates a sense of the numinous or awe. It continues to do this for me even after so many readings and so much study. I hope your study of the beatitudes assists in changing your brain and your worldview in such ways that you improve your conscious contact with yourself and the God of your understanding. To the best of our abilities, it is important to try to think like Christ. After all, we are striving for perfection, and He is our model and delivered the beatitudes to us as a guide.

The Blessings of the Beatitudes

There is a Chinese Proverb that goes something like this:

A farmer and his son had a beloved stallion that helped the family earn a living. One day, the horse ran away and their neighbors exclaimed, "Your horse ran away, what terrible luck!" The farmer replied, "Maybe yes, maybe no. We'll see."

A few days later, the horse returned home, leading a few wild mares back to the farm as well. The neighbors shouted out, "Your horse has returned, and brought several horses home with him. What great luck!" The farmer replied, "Maybe yes, maybe no. We'll see."

Figure 6: Hermeneutic Circle

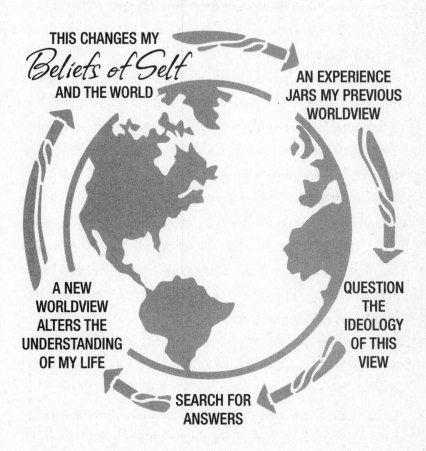

Figure 6: This figure is referred to as a "hermeneutic circle." It is a method that allows us to look at the existential questions of our life and through contemplation and/or meditation changes our beliefs about ourselves and about our world. This is a way we can read Jesus's words and reflect upon them. This model is adapted from the work of Juan Luis Segundo in *The Liberation of Theology*.

Later that week, the farmer's son was trying to break one of the mares and she threw him to the ground, breaking his leg. The villagers cried, "Your son broke his leg, what terrible luck!" The farmer replied, "Maybe yes, maybe no. We'll see."

A few weeks later, soldiers from the national army marched through town, conscripting all the able-bodied young men for the army. They did not take the farmer's son because of his injury. Friends shouted, "Your boy is saved, what incredible luck!" To which the farmer replied, "Maybe yes, maybe no. We'll see."

The moral of this story, is, of course, that no event, in and of itself, can truly be judged as good or bad, lucky or unlucky, fortunate or unfortunate, but that only time will tell the whole story. All is just consciousness flowing. Things are not always as they appear. There really is no duality of good or bad. It is "what is" and nothing more. The story of Solomon is an example of something that is not what it appears to be at face value. The interest is in where the situation leads you. Does it reinforce the ego or lead us to a better understanding of our true Self?

Solomon was the most magnificent king who ever lived. According to the world's standards, he had everything to make him happy. His wealth was immeasurable and his treasure so vast that the Old Testament says his silver was as common as rocks. He had fabulous food and stables with thousands of the finest horses in the world. Solomon had servants to wait on him and women by the hundreds. Yet his response to all of this was, "Vanity of vanities! All is vanity." (Ecclesiastes 1:2)

The word "blessed" comes from the Greek *makarios,* which basically means happy or blissful. It doesn't have anything to do with external circumstance. The best understanding is a description of someone who is blessed in himself and unaffected by outside contexts. This person is in harmony with all creation. Jesus's worldview was not concerned with politics and social structure. He was concerned about working on the inside of individuals . . . on our being. He understood that who we are determines what we think and do.

Sin is a refusal to admit we are nothing. We live for God and not our petty egos. An ego is in a constant state of becoming . . . a want or a desire to be something other than what it is. We suffer because we are caught up in ourselves. Sin is also a refusal to strive with all our might to realize the consciousness of the Christ within us.

Our need is to have God live in us and act in us. When this occurs, we constantly give love and receive love. This involves the emptying of self so in our nothingness we can constantly receive the full love of God. The ego wishes to appropriate this love toward itself. This narcissism causes isolation and conflict within us and with others. Suffering involves a reflection upon ourselves and how a situation has wronged us. Suffering comes from the experience of our own limitations and our self-centeredness.

Now we have the choice to either continue in our lack toward becoming some illusion or to surrender everything to God. We can turn back from the ego and move toward our original state of connectedness. When we have truly surrendered everything and the ego is depleted, there is no more suffering and misery. We can experience pain and fear, but, in the depths of our Christ-consciousness, we are at peace. We are no longer divided. I believe this is the nature of Jesus Christ on the cross.

The ego sees death as an evil to be avoided at all costs. Getting old is averted by plastic surgery and a lot of makeup. But when we have truly surrendered everything to God, death is a sacrament and a passage into eternal life.

Jesus Christ gave us the narrow road. I often wonder why there are so few on this way. Then again, I know nothing of God's larger plan. Maybe I am seeing life as seventy years and not seeing it as eternal. Evolution is creation manifesting itself over millions of years or more. It is very easy to be short-sighted.

There is the path to Christ, and it is open to individual interpretation. The first fifty or more times I read the Sermon on the Mount, the beatitudes seemed to have little depth to me. I then studied Hinduism, Buddhism, and the Tao. Since coming back to Contemplative Christianity, my understanding of the beatitudes has deepened. The following represents my understanding. It is important to contemplate this narrow road to Christ for yourself. Meditate upon it in silence and solitude.

Jesus states his objective at the beginning of the Sermon on the Mount, telling us we can know real blessedness, joy, happiness, and Divine reward. He continues by telling us the kind of character we need to develop to achieve these blessings. This is the story line of the beatitudes.

How to Utilize the Beatitudes

I understand that everyone has their own strengths and interests. Some like to meditate while others are more contemplative. There are some who utilize both strategies. Silence and solitude and prayer can be mixed and matched with contemplation and meditation. I don't believe there is a universal "right way." Find your own way. Find your own rhythm. Enter the flow of consciousness.

The following are my thoughts about the best ways to utilize what will be described in regard to the beatitudes. Remember, there is both a horizontal and vertical awareness that comes from studying the blessings. Think of them like the steps of a self-help group (that is, like the 12 Steps of Alcoholics Anonymous, Narcotics Anonymous, Gamblers Anonymous, and all related groups). We study the beatitudes from one through eight, but we do not stop there as we continue to work with each beatitude to delve deeply into their esoteric nature and define what this means to us. Over time, the meaning will flower, and the more you work with these blessings, the more you become them.

- **Read about each beatitude:** Notice if a sentence, statement, or paragraph captures your attention. If so, contemplate its meaning to your life. Apply this to your life and situation. The beatitudes are Jesus's personal message to you if you have ears to hear and eyes to see.

- **Listen to your thoughts as you read or during contemplation, meditation, silence and solitude, or during prayer:** It is what comes out of your heart that defines us. Pay attention to your thoughts as they indicate to you whether the ego is acting or Christ-consciousness (refer back to Chapter 4 for specific instructions). The egoic thoughts are those related to character defects such as:

1. Pride
2. Greed
3. Envy
4. Jealousy
5. Lust
6. Gluttony
7. Anger
8. Sloth
9. Judgmentalism
10. Self-Centeredness
11. Being Resentful
12. Prejudice
13. Self-Pity
14. Self-Righteousness
15. Impatience
16. Perfectionism

This is a partial list of character defects. Monitor your thoughts and reformulate into Christ-consciousness statements or surrender the defect to God. Learn to listen carefully to yourself and change your mind. As you change your mind, you change the physical brain.

Listen for any thoughts that are egoic in nature. The anger and resentment that comes from the belief "I cannot do what is required of me" or the self-pity of feeling sorry for ourselves as we look at how far we need to travel on the narrow road. Identify the defect of character and surrender it to God. I use a statement such as, "I surrender this defect of character to Thee, Oh Lord."

- **Reformulate the thoughts in your mind into Christ-consciousness statements.** For example change "I can never fulfill the requirements of this beatitude" into "I strive to the best of my abilities to fulfill the requirements of Christ-consciousness." Other useful thoughts for reprogramming are, "I can do nothing of my own, but with God all things are possible," "It all belongs to God," or "Give me strength and courage to do your will."

- **We are what originates from our heart.** If we want to achieve Christ-consciousness, we need to think and act like it.

- **Utilize contemplation and meditation to deepen and personalize the experience of the beatitude.** I like to put notes about each beatitude on an index card and at various times during the day read the card and contemplate some aspect of it, asking, "What does this mean to me?" "How can I apply this beatitude to my life today?" and "What do I need to work on?" One might utilize a traditional Benedictine practice of reading the beatitude, meditating upon it, and prayer intended to create an inner movement of communion with Christ. This is called *Lectio Divina* and has four steps. First you read, then follow the reading with meditation and prayer. Then contemplate the passage to help increase your knowledge of God's Word. In *Lectio Divina,* we enter into the beatitude with Christ in search of His consciousness.

- **Remember the passage "Therefore, you become perfect, just as your Father in heaven is perfect."** (Matthew 5:48). The word *perfect* also means "whole" as in "become a whole person." Remember, sin involves not becoming that which you truly are . . . a whole person.

- **Remember Jesus was not a teacher of theology and His teachings are of a spiritual or metaphysical nature.** It is what's beneath the words or what the words signify that is important. God is spirit, and He must be worshiped and understood in Spirit and in Truth.

An Inner Attitude of Receptivity and Openness

*Blessed are the humble, for theirs
is the Kingdom of Heaven.*

Jesus, a man who broke no laws and abided by all the rules of his religion, died between two criminals, was betrayed by a friend, and was rejected by religious and public authority. He showed us it is more important to be true to your faith than it is to be liked and respected by those held in high regard by most of the populous. In his humility, he shamed everyone.

Humility is to know that I am nothing and know nothing and to know this nothingness is everything because God resides in me and of me and is me. In my poverty of spirit, I am constantly emptying myself to be filled with the Holy Spirit.

To be "poor in spirit" is to empty myself of desires to exercise willpower. It is to start again and learn life as a child.

The important thing for us to consider is what this means to you and me in regard to how we are expected to live our lives. *To be humble is to be poor in spirit. To be poor in spirit means to empty ourselves completely of the false self so we can be filled with the spirit of God. This is the foundation from which all other beatitudes are built upon.*

I have used the metaphor of climbing a mountain in regard to attaining spiritual consciousness. We are told we have to ascend this mountain, and we try and try again but are not able to accomplish the task. We use all of our worldly resources and still fall short. From these experiences, we humble ourselves and come to the understanding we cannot accomplish this alone but need help. We are now poor in spirit and humble ourselves before God, asking for guidance and assistance.

Consider being poor in spirit as not being possessed by the magnetism of the material world. All of our money, connections, and scientific instruments cannot get us to the top. It does not mean we have to live the life of an aesthetic in abject poverty. What Jesus Christ is concerned about is our attitude toward our self and our capabilities. This is the antithesis of self-reliance and self-confidence. If you face up to God and view with wonder the world you live in, how can you experience anything but utter poverty?

In the wonderful book *Spirituality and the Beatitudes: Matthew's Vision for the Church in an Unjust World*, Michael Crosby states, "In this sense Matthew's 'poor in spirit' (ptochoi to pneumatic) represent neither a particular social or economic class nor people suffering from actual physical want, but those disciples who hear Jesus' teaching about the will of God, understand its implications in the depths of their being and put it into practice by good deeds of justice toward the poor. Those who realize their own need to reorder their lives toward God and who dedicate their lives to working for a reordering of God's creation are poor in spirit. In the depth of their being, at the core of their lives, their lives bear witness to their wholehearted dedication to God, to God's will, and to God's work. Matthew's vision of the reign of God given to the 'poor in spirit' is predicated on relationships and resources being ordered in the manner that fulfills God's plan."

The poor in spirit acknowledge God as the all-powerful who gives meaning to their lives. This is a pearl of great price, leading one to let go of anything else that has controlled one's life up until this point. "Letting go and letting God" is the emptying of oneself (kenosis) and being totally open to the mind of Jesus Christ. All spiritual disciplines, including the 12 Steps of Alcoholics Anonymous, require aspirants go through this process of "letting go" in order to be transformed.

Being poor in spirit does not mean we lack courage and are weak and diffident. It also does not mean living our life like Uriah Heep. Uriah Heep is the fictional character created by Charles Dickens in his classic *David Copperfield*. Heep, the moneylender, is the proverbial "yes man" frequently making references to his own humbleness when, in fact, he is patronizing, insincere, obsequious, and nauseating. All of this to cover his character defects of ambition, guile, and greed. There is no contrivance in humility as it is pureness of character.

Being poor in spirit also does not mean you have to make great personal sacrifices. You do not have to flog or starve yourself. Humility has nothing to do with behavior and everything to do with pureness of character. It is being conscious of our own insufficiency and inadequacy. The greatest biblical example of this is the Apostle Paul as he speaks in the book of Romans:

For I do not know what I do:
And I do not do the thing which I want,
But I do the thing which I hate.
That is exactly what I do.
So then if I do that which I do not wish to do,
I can testify concerning the law that it is good.
Now then it is not I who do it,
But sin which dominates me.
Yet I know that it does not fully dominate me, (that is in my flesh)
But as far as good is concerned,
The choice is easy for me to make,
But to do it, that is difficult.

—ROMANS 7:15–18

Poverty should never be idealized. In the material sense, it is neither a condition necessary for salvation nor an obstruction to it. Salvation is given to people who are poor in themselves, not poor in material possessions. Possessions become problematic when we become addicted or attached to them—when we put too much energy into people, places, and things and take energy away from our spiritual growth, worship of God, and from loved ones. Part of our worship is giving of ourselves to others in need. The 12 Steps of Alcoholics Anonymous give us a contemporary parallel to the beatitudes as the "steps" confront issues of control, speak of spiritual conversion, service to others, and bringing the message of hope to those in need.

Jesus said, "I can do nothing of myself." It is God who does the work. If Jesus could do nothing of his own, this surely must make us feel hopeless regarding our own powers. This should certainly lead us to an understanding of the need for total submission. There is a complete absence of pride and of self-assurance. It is to admit our nothingness . . . that there is absolutely nothing we can do of ourselves to reach the top of the mountain. That is to be poor of spirit.

In *Studies in the Sermon on the Mount*, Martyn Llyoyd-Jones wrote, "It means this, that if we are truly Christians we shall not rely upon our natural birth. We shall not rely upon the fact that we belong to certain families; we shall not boast that we belong to certain nations or nationalities. We shall not build upon our natural temperament. We shall not believe in or rely upon our natural position in life, or any powers that may have been given to us. We shall not rely upon money or any wealth we may have. The thing about which we shall boast will not be the education we have received, or the particular school or college to which we may have been. No, all that is what Paul came to regard as 'dung', and a hindrance to this greater thing because it tended to master and control him." There is nothing about ourselves that is persuasive in regard to being humble. Humility or being poor of spirit is a diminution of all that we are. It is the ultimate realization that we own nothing, have nothing, are nothing, and are utterly dependent upon God's grace for all we enjoy. Feel the emptiness and understand it as a prerequisite to wholeness.

I humbly surrender everything to Thee Oh Lord
for I am nothing without you.

Vulnerable and Reaching Out for What We Lost

Blessed are they who mourn, for
they shall be comforted.

The material world does not bless those who mourn. These are people to be avoided at all cost. They are truly "bummers." There is something definitely wrong with them. That is where Valium, Librium, and the Heinz's 57 variety of tranquilizers and other drugs come in. "Be happy at all costs," the world says.

There are times when "eat, drink, and be merry" fail us. We are a nation of anxious people partly because we refuse to look at the truth about ourselves and the world we live in. The cognitive dissonance between "what is" and what we "want it to be" creates a world full of distress.

Love is distorted by selfish desires to cling to ephemeral or illusory happiness. By giving up these illusions, we learn we can live without what we previously thought to be essential. We learn not to make external pleasures into idols.

If we spend all of our time trying to find happiness, there is little or no time to realize our transgressions. We might get counseling or read a book if we feel anxious and depressed instead of mourning our own sin. Some will deny there is a problem trying to project an air of faultlessness. We can both deny and put on a phony front for all to see or admit it and sink into despair. Better yet, admit it and turn to God for mercy and grace. God will comfort us but not in the way the world desires. No frills, just a sense of abiding peace and hope in the midst of despair.

We must come to God with a bankrupt spirit, mourning our transgressions. This has nothing to do with egoic self-pity and everything to do with the spiritual aspect of our beings. It has to do with being comforted. Happiness comes to you not because of your sorrow but because this sorrow leads to comfort. Jesus invites us to such comfort in Matthew 11:28 when he states, "Come to me, all you who are tired out and carrying burdens, and I will give you rest." The mission of

Jesus was to comfort sinners with the understanding that a day of peace is coming.

Jesus bore the depths of our mourning. He took on our tears and brokenness, our anxiety, depression, and loneliness, and He alleviated our guilt, rejection, and isolation. In return, He comforts us with peace, acceptance, and restoration and gives us a new sense of meaning and mission in life.

To receive His comfort (the Presence of God), we must first learn to mourn. For many, denial keeps us from admitting the exact error of our ways. Without honest admission, we will never take the necessary steps toward our deliverance. Most will not take the time and expend the energy needed to learn the Truth until some personal tragedy occurs in their lives. Marital discord, business failure, legal complications, and problems such as alcoholism and addiction need not occur in our lives if we seek first Christ-consciousness. However, failing to do so leads to spiritual opportunities disguised as tragedy. These opportunities can lead one to be comforted.

Going a step further, to believe you are saved just because you belong to the right group or church is delusional. Any nation or religion that believes they "have God on their side" is like the Pharisees who were rejected by Jesus. Spiritual pride hardens the heart and leaves no room for Christ-consciousness. In Alcoholics Anonymous, one takes a 4th Step by listing all of the "sins" of the past and then a 5th Step where this is shared with their Higher Power (who already knows) and with another human being. This forces one to face their innermost self and to acknowledge their mourning. The pride of the ego is dealt a lethal blow.

As I consider Jesus and try to understand His standards, which I am expected to live up to, I am overwhelmed with helplessness. This leaves me poor in spirit. I mourn the fact that my sinful condition is so far removed from expectations. I mourn also for the dreadful condition of the world and all those struggling with the temptations of life. However, I am hopeful and comforted because this mourning leads to sorrow and atonement. A man who truly and honestly examines himself cannot help but mourn. Contemplation will lead one to the conclusion so well described by the Apostle Paul in Romans 7:18:

But as far as good is concerned,
The choice is easy for me to make,
But to do it, that is difficult.

Spiritual mourning is different from the type we experience with the death of a loved one. This is a type of selfish sorrow experienced by the loss of something or someone we believe we will have difficulty living without. It is a worldly mourning. The variety of mourning we are speaking of is spiritual mourning. Mourning creates an emptiness, allowing for the touch of Divine compassion and the fullness of the Spirit. First, we must mourn, then we can be comforted. We must humbly understand our spiritual situation and look to God for solution. The problem is, we struggle mightily with our pride instead of admitting we cannot accomplish a solution alone. The resolution is a Divine one—the comfort received from Jesus, the Holy Spirit, and God.

I believe Jesus mourned because He saw the evil so clearly in people, and he understood their lack of awareness of their true Self. He, like the Buddha, saw the suffering caused by the human ego. Like Jesus and the Buddha, we mourn because of the very pervasive nature of the ego in the world and all of its terrible tragedies and cruelty.

Jesus Christ told us the man who truly mourns the spiritual condition of himself and the world he lives in is in the process of repenting. When one is repentant, this leads him toward the solution, which is Jesus. As we start to know the truth and receive more Light in our lives, it creates both energy and a state of joy. Seeing oneself and the world as it really is, without rose-colored glasses, or the filters of the ego, certainly makes one feel the hopelessness of this world's situation. All governments have failed. Our education and knowledge are not leading us out of the wickedness of the world. Our world seems to be getting more narcissistic as time goes by. It is all about "me," but my personal ways don't work. The League of Nations failed and so is the United Nations.

Our joy then must come from the belief in a world to come. Without the hope of enlightenment—a new birth leading to a new heaven and earth, what is there to be elated about? Without radical spiritual change, there is no hope in the world we live in. Nothing that has been tried to date to relieve suffering and create equality has worked.

Martyn Lloyd-Jones best defines a man who spiritually mourns in *Studies in the Sermon on the Mount*, stating, "He is a sorrowful man, but he is not morose. He is a serious man, but he is not a solemn man. He is sober-minded, but he is not a sullen man. He is a grave man, but he is never cold or prohibitive. . . . No, no; he is a man who looks at life seriously; he contemplates it spiritually, and he sees in it sin and its effects." This kind of man can enter into solidarity with the corruption and pain in this world while not needing rose-colored glasses.

How difficult this is. We should not lose our self in depression or anxiety but realize the blessing of comfort offered to us in mourning. I try to detach (not unattached or nonattachment because this would leave me cold) from myself and the world. The ability to detach, or to stand back from, and contemplate my life and the disarray of the world and to know the perfection of Jesus Christ are what is demanded of me and leaves out any influence of the ego. To witness the Truth—the disparity between my thoughts and actions versus what they should be or to see the cruelty in this world versus what this world could be like—gives me a sense of deep mourning. I am nothing and cannot do anything to save the world or myself other than to admit my helplessness to my Creator, who I ask to direct my life.

Lord, give me the courage and strength to
be your messenger and your servant.

Taming the Egoic Instincts

Blessed are the meek, for they
shall inherit the earth.

The meek are those who do not get angry in the face of insult or injury. They are taking apart their need to try to control people, places, and things. Because they have worked on acceptance, they are nonjudgmental. The meek even refuse to injure others in spite of provocation, understanding the ways of the ego and of the world of which they often do not approve but, even so, do not make judgments.

Judge not, and you will not be judged;
Condemn not, and you will not be condemned;
Forgive, and you shall be forgiven.

—LUKE 6:37

They are able to have compassion for those still stuck in the need for power and control. This is not a passive attitude but one revealing a true understanding of love. It is like *Ahisma,* the practice of nonviolence made famous by Gandhi.

Being meek has nothing whatsoever to do with a lack of courage. A meek person is gentle with a subdued character. It is power that one has under control. It comes for a self-emptying, self-humiliating brokenness before God. Being meek helps one understand where the power really is.

A meek person doesn't get angry when wrong is perpetrated against him. He doesn't even defend himself because he knows he doesn't deserve anything. Meekness says, "I can do nothing of my own but through God everything is possible." There is a perfect willingness to allow God's will to come about and not our own.

Meekness gives God the glory. It exhibits self-control without getting angry or reacting to perceived slights. How difficult it is to not react when others are criticizing or insulting you. In these situations, I often tell people they are entitled to their own opinion.

A meek person does come forth when God is dishonored, however. Here we must stand up for Truth. In all situations, the meek person makes peace and forgives, restoring order all around him.

The presence of humility, mourning, and meekness dramatically reduces the power and control of the ego. The diminution of the ego alienates one from the masses. You don't fit in anymore. You now belong to a very different kingdom. You are in this world but not of it. Now you are at the point where you become genuinely concerned about other people—not concerned about others because of how it might impact you, but truly concerned regardless of how it impacts you.

Meekness is saying the Truth when telling a lie would go over so much better. It does not compromise. For the spiritual aspirant, the first three beatitudes leave no room for compromise. It is an all-or-nothing proposition. You are either humble, or you are not. You are either meek, or you are not.

There must be an absence of pride in order to be meek. Pride is the frontman for the ego. Some speak of false pride while I say all pride is false. By nature, it is an egoic defense against its opposite—meekness and humility. If I say, "I am proud of myself for not being as bad a person as Joseph," what am I really saying? I am comparing and contrasting myself with another to alleviate inferior feelings when not living up to a standard. Perfection is a very difficult standard. That's why I mourn.

There is no self-pity in the person who is truly meek. To be meek truly means one is beyond personal sensitivity. One has come to the realization that nothing in this material world can truly harm him. He is free.

No longer worry about living up to some standard unless it is God's. What do I have to protect myself from? Is it the slings and arrows of others who place themselves so far above me and are proud of it? There is nothing here worthy of defense. Being meek is being totally finished with feeling sorry for me. We waste so much time in self-pity. I am amazed that people think as high of me as they do for I have done so little to deserve it.

A person who feels he doesn't deserve anything will always be content. He will always be satisfied and is already gratified. For to have nothing is to have everything and to be empty allows He who bought us with such a heavy price to enter us fully. This is the Presence of Christ-consciousness living through us.

John MacArthur in his lovely book *The Beatitudes: The Only Way to Happiness* states, "We cannot help ourselves. We are hopeless. We are sinful. And that is followed by, 'they that mourn.' That is the response to your broken spirit: mourning. Then there is meekness, and meekness says 'In comparison to God, I am nothing!' Meekness is humility. In our meekness before God, we realize that the only hope we ever have of knowing righteousness is to seek it at His hand. That brings us to the fourth beatitude, and we hunger and thirst after what we know is not ours."

Although a project of many lifetimes, the ego and its defects of character should be diminishing as the experience of the first three beatitudes are personally and honestly internalized. This is the vertical aspect of living the beatitudes. Some changes you might notice are captured in the following table:

Table 5. Changes Observed from Internalizing the First Three Beatitudes

I USED TO BE	NOW I AM
Prideful	Humble
Greedy	Altruistic
Lustful	Consensual sharing
Angry	Gentle
Gluttonous	Disciplined
Envious and jealous	Grateful
Judgmental	Accepting

Table 5: As you practice the beatitudes and start to understand the deeper esoteric meanings, you should start to hear yourself (your self-talk and overt conversation) take on a very different tone. This table shows some of the changes you should be observing. Remember, this practice is never over, and the more you work toward Christ-consciousness, the more you will hunger for it.

The first three beatitudes move us to look deeply inside ourselves. We are to clean out the conditioned ego and make room for greater Light and Christ-consciousness.

Lord, this is all I want . . .
to get as close to you as I possibly can
and to know your ways.

Connecting to the Force Field
of Christ-Consciousness

Blessed are those who hunger and thirst for justice,
for they shall be well satisfied.

All of us are created with a hunger for God. This is a hunger for holiness and Truth. Unfortunately, this hunger becomes diverted by the ego into a longing for material things. When this happens, suffering is inevitable.

If we are truly mourning, humble, and meek, this hunger is now properly directed. This beatitude then changes the course from the problem to the solution. The problem was we were not "poor in spirit," were not meek, and did not understand Truth, which leads to mourning. However, as we contemplate the first three beatitudes, this leads us to the solution. It induces a hunger and thirst for righteousness.

We have been concerned with the difficulties of the ego, and now we can be concerned with an orderly mind and how to create a quality of life we have not known since infancy. The feeling of life flows as we connect to the Spirit. We long for salvation and understand it is entirely provided by grace as a free gift from God.

Mostly we have hungered for blessedness and happiness. However, this is why we never become at peace. We are looking for something that should not be sought as they are signs and not what is signified. They are the results of something else much more fundamental. It is in the seeking of righteousness that being blessed and being at peace come into our lives.

Now the question becomes, "What is righteousness?" Hungering and thirsting for righteousness means, in a general sense, the desire to be right with God. It means the desire to be free from sin and the misery caused by the ego. Sin and the many disguises of the ego have alienated us from God. We now long for our original relationship with The Father. Sin and rebellion have separated us from God, so with all our might, we continue to rid ourselves of the suffering and misery of the ego while through prayer, contemplation, and meditation, and, in a state of helplessness, we ask God for grace and strength.

In this human state of existence, there is now the driving desire to know God as much as possible. My prayers are always to ask God to let me come as close to an understanding of His ways as possible and for the courage and strength to take responsibility for this knowledge. It is the driving desire to walk in the Light . . . to be like Jesus Christ.

When we look at the hunger and the thirst for Christ-consciousness, we must remember that we cannot attain it on our own. The hunger goes on gaining intensity until it is satisfied. It becomes so intense as to sometimes be painful. One has to be desperate in their desire. Only by grace can this longing be fulfilled.

Grace allows us to go beyond the Old Testament karmic law of "an eye for an eye." In the New Testament, one follows the proclamation of Jesus Christ, who told us to love our neighbors as ourselves and to love God with everything we have. It is this intensity of love that is required as we hunger for righteousness and the grace of the Father.

We are all perfect—perfectly where we need to be to learn the lessons we are here to learn. There is the Presence and perfection of Christ-consciousness in all of us. However, the ego has gotten in the way. The beatitudes are a way toward realization of that perfection in each of us. It is an arduous, narrow road with no vacations, time off, or coffee breaks. It is a hungry, intense, and relentless search. The closer one gets to enlightenment, the stronger will be the pull of Christ-consciousness. In the home stretch, one becomes energized and tireless.

The realization of this perfection is being like Jesus Christ. Most seem to believe it means being a "good" person—decent and moral up to a certain point. I hope you have noticed the rigorous standards demanded if one wants to bring more Light into themselves. It is not just for you as your Light radiates into the world and impacts others. If we had enough Light in this world (if people of Light became the majority), all of the darkness of corruption would come to an end. Society would change and justice prevail.

At this point, if we are paying attention to our behaviors, thoughts, and emotions, we notice if we are moving toward the Light or away from it. On a day-by-day basis both voluntarily and deliberatively, we remind ourselves of our calling as spiritual beings. Is this way of life becoming the greatest desire of our life? Are we spending time in spiritual study? Are we utilizing the tools of contemplation, meditation, silence and solitude, and prayer? Are we feeling a mounting hunger for God's grace? Can you feel the intensity of spiritual energy?

Dear Lord, let me gain as much Light as you
will allow me to have in this lifetime.

Giving Is Receiving and Aligns the Universe

Blessed are the merciful, for
to them shall be mercy.

This beatitude is another turning point for the spiritual aspirant as we show ourselves as people of the Light and become merciful. This beatitude is related to the first where humility or being poor in spirit reveals us as beggars. We will be willing to show mercy to others who are begging for mercy. Mercy never holds a grudge, makes judgments, extracts vengeance, or takes advantage of others' weakness. It is like humility—you either have it or you don't. Faking it doesn't work. There is no selfish merit to be received by being merciful; it is its own reward.

Kind action coupled with unkind thinking is a form of deceit. It is motivated by character defects such as greed and motives such as to get a person to like me and/or give me what I want. I find it interesting when someone is trying to use me for their own gain and/or at my expense; I can feel them coming a mile away.

Let's first explore the meaning of being merciful. Many believe this means that if we are good to others they will be good to us. Unfortunately, the world does not work in this way. You can be merciful to the world, and the world can crucify you. In Roman times, being merciful was a sign of weakness. When a child was born, the father had the right of *patria protestas*. He decided if he wanted the newborn to live by a mere show of the thumb. Thumb up, the newborn lived. Thumb down, and the infant was immediately drowned. If a Roman did not want a slave, he could just kill him. Tired of his wife or looking for another, he could just kill her. No, the world doesn't show mercy. If mercy carried reward, Jesus would not have been crucified.

My interpretation of this is if we are merciful to everyone and every living thing, God will be merciful to us. So it is not the world we are worried about but our relationship with God. As John MacArthur states in *The Beatitudes: The Only Way to Happiness*, "We think of mercy so much in terms of forgiveness in salvation, but it is really a much broader term. It goes beyond sympathy. It means sympathy and compassion in action toward anyone in need. When our Lord talks about it here, the real *eliamosuna* (Greek for merciful) is not the weak sympathy that carnal selfishness feels but never does anything about. It is not the false mercy that indulges its own flesh in salving of conscience by giving tokenism. It is not the silent, passive pity that never seems to help in a tangible way. It is genuine compassion with the pure, unselfish motive that reaches out to help." Mercy is meeting the need, not just feeling what another is feeling and having empathy. Again, I am speaking of going behind the sign or symptom and dealing with the real cause of the problem. To feel someone's loneliness and have compassion is not enough. We must provide comfort and company even when we find the other's personality (character defects) irritating.

I believe we also must show mercy toward ourselves. As we move beyond the narcissistic aspects of the ego, we discover the illusion. We could never live up to the idealized image we have of ourselves. For many of us, the self-critical and perfectionistic aspects of our ego has been causing great suffering for so long.

By elimination—the emptying of self—we are now capable of receiving the mercy and love of Christ-consciousness. Mercy is now pouring out of us to others in need. As we empty ourselves, it creates the space for the Holy Spirit to add grace to our lives. We never run out of love and mercy, as the more we give the more we have.

If one lives a sinful life and never acknowledges one's sinfulness and fails to strive to achieve Christ-consciousness, there is no guarantee of God's mercy. God is the source of mercy, but only for those who are striving to live the beatitudes. To receive the unlimited mercy of God, we must be humble, meek, and mournful while hungering and thirsting for righteousness.

At this point, I believe our actions result much more from intuition than thought. At this stage, the Presence is working through us. It is

Christ-consciousness beginning to run our lives for us. The more ego we get out of the way, the more the Presence straightens out the highways for us. Rest in the Presence, as it always works from love and, as a result, will never steer you wrong.

Being merciful does not mean we should turn our heads to injustice. It does not mean to be easygoing and pretend we just do not see what is going on around us. In this time of anything goes and truth is relative to the beliefs of the individual, we all need to stand up for goodness and Truth. It seems to me with this expansive way of defining what is each person's truth—*not what is Truth*—people seem to be more anxious and depressed than ever before. When the ego sets the standards, it will always lead to more suffering and misery.

As you engage in the lifelong spiritual study of the beatitudes, you will notice marvelous changes in your worldview. You will not see people as you used to see them. Through the eyes of Christ-consciousness, acceptance and surrender allow us to see the perfection of God's plan, manifesting itself in everyone and everything. There are no longer people to dislike but people to be pitied as they are governed by the gods of this material world. We feel a sorrow for all of those who are helpless slaves to the sins of this world and cannot see a way out. This is in essence the test. Have we truly changed our view of the world and of the people in it? Are we more merciful and forgiving? Do we harbor grudges? Have I come to the point where I see men and women as victims of the material world? No one is bad, as we are all created by God. He only created the good. Can we see the good in others? Remember, we have a responsibility to those in need as the Christ in the other is calling out to us for assistance. Be merciful and give of your energy.

Lord, let me share your Light
with those in need.

A Heart Not Divided

Blessed are those who are pure in their hearts,
for they shall see God.

The wonderful metaphysical teacher Emmet Fox in his book *The Sermon on the Mount* states, "Blessed are they who recognize God as the only real Cause, and the only real Presence, and the only real Power; not merely in a theoretical or formal way, but practically, and specifically, and wholeheartedly, in all their thoughts, and words, and actions; and not merely in some parts of their lives, but in every nook and corner of their lives and mentalities, keeping nothing back from Him, but bringing their own wills in every last particular into perfect harmony with His Will—for they shall overcome all limitation of time, and space, and matter, and carnal mind; and realize and enjoy the Presence of God forever."

One might look at the beatitudes as a developmental model. The next beatitude is building upon the lessons of the previous. We can also look at the beatitudes as having different focuses and also as being interrelated. The first three beatitudes focus upon our recognition of need. We are poor in spirit, mourning our inability to be free of the ego, and meek because of an understanding of our worldly nature. The satisfaction of need is in the hungering and thirsting for righteousness. As a result of being filled with righteousness, we become merciful, pure in heart, and peacemakers. As we mourn our spiritual condition, understanding our nothingness, we realize the fact that only God can help us become pure of heart. When we sincerely mourn the impurity of our heart and surrender to God totally, He can cleanse our heart and make it pure and single-minded in purpose—to love God with all our heart, mind, strength, and spirit and to desire only to do His will.

*Dear Lord, help me to be your servant
and your messenger.*

To have purity of heart is to have singleness of purpose. It is to wish for one thing and that is a relationship with the Father through the creation of our Christ-consciousness. You might notice at this point that the only thing of great value is to strengthen this relationship with all our might.

Let's look at what the heart meant in the time of Jesus Christ. The heart was considered the center of one's personality. Everything comes from the heart—our emotions, thoughts, and behaviors. All of our troubles arise from the heart. To have an impure heart meant to have a conflict between the right thoughts, feelings, and actions and those of the materialistic ego.

The Pharisees and legalists of Jesus's day were more concerned with rules and laws governing the external self. They were concerned about rituals and not so concerned about "cleansing the inside of the cup." The hypocrisy of the Pharisees involved their attentions to external laws while their hearts were full of iniquity.

The beatitude reads that one with a pure heart will see God. It doesn't mean that if I am a decent and moral human being I will see God. The requirements are much more stringent. If I want to see God, I must have a pure heart full of Light in which no darkness resides. This is a heart that is fixed in its devotion and has pure motivation. We cannot accomplish this on our own. Only an indwelling of the Holy Spirit can clean our heart. This happens in the crucible where we come to commune with God and to beg for Divine intervention.

I pray to Thee, Oh Father, to let me come as close to you as possible, to achieve the consciousness of Christ.

Trying to be pure of heart goes against the beliefs of the material world. If you strive and pray, meditate, and contemplate what a pure single-focused heart means to you and notice how your behaviors, thoughts, and feelings change, you will also notice you will become unpopular in most circles. The only support you will get is by surrounding yourself with holy company. However, your purity of heart is meant to shine everywhere so expect it to cause others to either avoid or condemn you because of how you make them feel on the inside. This dissonance is caused by the others' conflict between who they are and what they know they should be. The degree of this conflict is based upon the level of their spiritual consciousness.

We will be tempted by impure thoughts and do things that violate our beliefs. Our mind will also have impure egotistical motives. That is why paying attention to your mind is so important. If we can stop the impure thought or motive before its energy is delivered into emotion and behavior, we can intervene and then correct our negative thinking. If we continually do this, the old patterns of thinking, behaving, and feeling will gradually go away as new brain circuits are developed based upon pureness of heart and mind. Remember though, you cannot accomplish this totally on your own but can only do this by faith. Purity of the heart will make God visible to you. You will see the world through the lens of Christ-consciousness. You will see the reflection of God in the perfection of His creation.

Inner Peace Flowing into the World

_Blessed are the peacemakers, for they
shall be called sons of God._

To be a peacemaker, one must give up all alliance with the ego. More specifically, we must give up the need to control. It is not a matter of doing it your way, as it needs to be done God's way. To surrender the need for control is to finally admit that God does not need our help. Everything is according to His plan. He is doing just fine without our compulsive and ineffective need to change people, places, and things. Our worldview must change accordingly, allowing us to see the perfection of God's creation and the understanding we all are perfectly where we need to be to learn the lessons we are here to learn in this lifetime. This can be expanded to accept ourselves as we are. Now we are in a position to be peacemakers.

Whether we are talking about parents, relational partners, or countries, we have to end the attempt to try to make others in our own image. We need to make sure "could have" and "should be" are out of our vocabulary. We need to accept ourselves and others just as we and they are; not as how we might want us and them to be. To be a peacemaker, we must go to others (our partners, neighbors, other countries, etc.) in a state of affirmation of caring. We then share our concerns without telling the other what they need to do, think, or feel. The other will know deep inside if you are sincere, and your sincerity will greatly influence their decision.

Once we have established peace within ourselves, we can become a servant of creation. Peacemakers are, in a sense, God acting in the world. It is Divine Empowerment. Peacemakers are God's agents operating in the material world.

The world's politicians and other arbitrators of peace have a miserable track record. As John MacArthur states in *The Beatitudes: The Only Way to Happiness*, "Peace is merely that brief glorious moment in history when everybody stops to reload. The world was concerned in the aftermath of World War II with developing an agency for world peace, so in 1945 the United Nations brought itself into existence with the motto: 'To have succeeding generations free from the scourge of war.' Since that time there has not been one day of peace on the earth. Not one. It's a pipe dream." Because man has no peace inside himself, the world, which is a projection of the inner heart of man, is full of turmoil.

Peacemakers transcend the emotions. They do not use force but live out the personage God made them to be. They are living the Truth of God's Kingdom. There can only be peace when the world does not rest on lies and deceit. Unfortunately, in our world today, we do not even expect our elected officials to tell us the truth.

Peacemakers stand up for Truth. Peacemaking is reconciliation. It involves learning how to live with those who may despise us while trying to get earth to mirror the Kingdom of God. Peace often begins with conflict.

Do not expect that I have come to bring peace on earth;
I have not come to bring peace but a sword.

—MATTHEW 10:34

A peacemaker is all about Truth. He is also about standing up for this Truth even when it creates conflict. Conflict can only be resolved if we start from the Truth. Any other way complicates the conflict, making it worse in the long run. Peace can only come when the Truth is known. In your life if you have righteousness, Truth, and holiness, you will have peace. The menaces to peace are those who spread lies and deceit. When you are a righteous person, you have peace with God and with yourself. What else is important?

Having an undivided heart is to be pure in your heart. It is to know Truth . . . not the world's truth but Divine Truth. It is this undivided Truth in the heart that produces a peacemaker. When you become a peacemaker, the world caught up in the lies of the ego will refuse to accept you. They do not want to hear about the peace God has to offer as the dissonance creates pain and anxiety.

If you are a peacemaker, you will divide people, you will disturb them, and you will disrupt the relative comfort created by the illusions of the ego. We stand for the Truth even when it disturbs others. Therefore, to be a peacemaker is not to be an easygoing people pleaser. There must be conviction and a sense of righteousness to stand for Truth. To stand for Truth is to stand against the selfishness, self-centeredness, and vanity of the world. The ego is the cause of all of the world's problems. You cannot be successful only treating the symptoms, and there will be no peace until the collective ego is overcome. A peacemaker then is one who wishes for all men to reconcile with God.

This world does not want to hear the peacemaker. Fortunately, you will find some people and small groups that do. This is where the energy of Truth can flourish and the Word can be spread. Just remember, the world is like those passersby when Jesus was on the cross. They mocked him and cursed him. In Roman times, as in our time, we honor those who gain power and wealth by any means. We have become a whole culture of people looking for our fifteen minutes of fame so we can exalt ourselves. Our nation's motto should be, "What's in it for me?" In this kind of atmosphere, a righteous person will have to pay the price. A peacemaker will have to endure attempts to belittle and invalidate. In all the turmoil of the world, we must be an eye in the storm and a beacon for peace. We are to reconcile—to bring peace into the world.

And all things have become new through God
Who has reconciled us to himself by Jesus Christ,
And has given to us the ministry of reconciliation;
For God was in Christ,
Who has reconciled the world with his majesty,
Not counting their sins against them;
And has committed to us the word of reconciliation.
Now then we are ambassadors for Christ,
As though God did beseech you by us;
We beseech you for Christ;
Be reconciled to God.

—2 CORINTHIANS 18–20.

First we must make peace with God and then we can become His peace corp. If we are truly at peace with ourselves and with God, now we can bring this peace to the world in our relationships, including those who were, at one time, our enemies.

Lord, work through me and shine the
Light of peace into the darkness.

Pure Liberation, Freedom, and Illumination

Blessed are those who are persecuted for the
sake of justice, for theirs is the kingdom of heaven.
Blessed are you, when they reproach you, and
speak against you every kind of bad word, falsely,
for my sake, then be glad and rejoice, for
your reward is increased in heaven.

In the days of Caesar, once a year every person in the empire had to burn incense to him and decree, "Caesar is lord." After burning the incense, those who made this decree were given a certificate called a *libellus,* allowing them to worship any god they wanted. Christians would not say anything except "Jesus is Lord." They never received a certificate and, therefore, were worshiping illegally. For this, they were always facing torture.

Some prefer to split this beatitude into two separate ones. I believe the beatitude is "Blessed are those who are persecuted for the sake of justice, for theirs is the kingdom of heaven." The rest is a condition attached to the beatitude. It speaks of the various forms of injustice and how this will increase your reward in heaven.

At this stage of spiritual development, one has developed wisdom and total humility and is a "nobody." Did you ever think you would rejoice at being an absolute nobody? At this level of spiritual consciousness, one is detached from all worldly goods. There is no willingness to compromise one's Self, and there is no price high enough to consider selling one's soul. One is totally beyond self-interest and at peace with the world. When we are pouring out Divine Light into the universe, we will certainly bump up against the ways of the egoic world. I remember Dr. Martin Luther King saying, "If you haven't found something that is worth dying for, you haven't found anything worth living for."

When we are persecuted, there is no ego in you to fight back. It takes two to fight, and it takes two for one to be right and one to be wrong. It takes two for one to win and the other to lose. When they cannot find "you" anywhere, there is no ego, no duality, and no competition. If we do not fight, nor do we compete, the one who persecutes us with words does not get what he is looking for. Without an argument, there is no fuel to add to the hatred.

With total acceptance of "what is," we see the other(s) for who they really are. We look at them through the eyes of Christ-consciousness.

We may mourn for their misery, but we do not retaliate. If the opportunity presents, we teach.

When we hunger and thirst for righteousness and a right relationship with God and receive Light (Truth), some of those who come into contact with us are going to be contentious. Those who have achieved a high degree of Christ-consciousness stand for the Truth and put out a high level of spiritual energy. This alone will have an impact on others in your vicinity. For those seeking righteousness, it can have a positive, even healing, effect. For those who are ego bound, it will create a degree of dissonance, making them feel a negative emotion such as anger or anxiety. One way of dealing with these negative feelings is to discount or put down the righteous person. In these situations when God is attacked, we stand up for Truth. If the attack is toward us as an individual, there is literally no one there to attack and, therefore, no one left to counter the attack. The righteous is never fanatical or overzealous.

This beatitude does not say we will be rewarded when we suffer for a human cause. Sometimes the two can be one. There is no reward when we suffer for a political/religious cause. When the two are mixed, it will usually lead to trouble. We have to be able to discriminate between political prejudices and spiritual principles. I think the best way to think about this is to understand that being righteous is trying our best to be like Jesus Christ and suffering in this world because of it. This harassment can come from the church itself when one is spiritual and not dogmatic. We are persecuted because we are different.

The human mind or ego does not align with God. It seeks its own power for personal gain and aggrandizement. As we gather Light, the ego diminishes, and we start to become more Christ-like; a rebirth is necessary to become righteous. I believe the following, as stated by Lloyd-Jones in his book *Studies in the Sermon on the Mount*, beautifully explains this process: "To become like Him we have to become light; light always exposes darkness, and the darkness therefore always hates the light. We are not to be offensive; we are not to be foolish; we are not to be unwise; we are not even to parade the Christian faith. We are not to do anything that calls for persecution. But by just being like Christ persecution becomes inevitable. But that is a glorious thing." Later in his book, Lloyd-Jones describes the types of persecution we might face when he states, "It can take the form of men actually being shot, or murdered in some other way. It may take the form of a man losing his post. It may manifest itself just by sneering and jeering and laughter as he enters the room. It may take the form of a kind of whispering campaign. There is no end to the ways the persecuted may suffer. But that is not what matters. What really matters is the way in which the Christian faces these things."

We face persecution without any retaliation at all. At its best, there is even no thought of retribution. It is soundest to manage the situation by finding the familiar space in the moment we have grown to know so well in our silence and solitude, prayer, and meditation. In this space, there is no depression that might occur if we start to judge ourselves or others. Remember, only God should pass judgment.

Maybe the most difficult aspect is to get past the ego's tendency to form resentment. As previously mentioned, resentment gives us permission to do anything we want because somebody else made us do it. Whether real or perceived, this situation leads to a negative emotional state such as anger, prejudice, anxiety, depression, and so on. If we experience resentment, it allows us to do anything we want because "It is their fault not mine." We can get angry and retaliate, spread false rumors, or play hurtful pranks. We can go out and hurt ourselves by spending money we don't have on a credit card, eat something we know we shouldn't, and use alcohol or drugs or any other self-defeating behavior. Although outwardly ridiculous, it felt right at the time. Later on, we feel remorse and beat ourselves up. This is unresolved spiritual pride and lets us know that we still have work to do.

It is important to examine why we are joyful about being persecuted for righteousness. We are not happy about being tormented. Nor should we think we are better than those who persecute us. We should be exceedingly glad because it is evidence our life has become like His. We rejoice because our reward will be in the afterlife.

Lord, give me the courage and strength to do
your will despite the consequences.

Summary

There are certain understandings that guide those with Christ-consciousness. The first is our difference from those who are caught up in the "go go" world of materialistic desires. We no longer live for our ego and prefer to rest in God. If we are in faith, living in the moment, and not obsessed with "the next great thing," we will receive what we need. Lastly, we do not need to think of the future or fear death while the ego-driven person does everything he can to not think of death and eternity. I believe our culture with its many toys and thrills is built to keep these fears at bay.

There is a manifest world and an unmanifest world. It is only one entity with the manifest being the visible realm and the unmanifest the invisible. Think of faith as the door between the manifest and the unmanifest. When we have faith, our needs are drawn from the energy of the unmanifest and made visible and available to us in the manifest. As we develop greater degrees of Christ-consciousness, this door becomes easier to find, as well as to open. To be in faith is to be in the moment, understanding our needs will be met by a gracious God.

The beatitudes are the narrow road to enlightenment that Jesus Christ taught. Jesus tells us, "As I am, you, too, must become." He will always be there for us, but we must do the work. Jesus Christ is the "Life Giver" (Mahyana) and the "Unified or Enlightened One" (Ihidaya). He gives us a path and is the giver of eternal life. The path points us in the right direction. Enlightenment is a journey into the unknown and is a very personal journey one takes alone, or I might say with the God of their understanding.

Cynthia Bourgeault describes this path to *metanoia* (repentance, to go "beyond the mind" or "into the larger mind") in her book *The Wisdom Jesus* as, "In these eight familiar sayings we can now see that Jesus is talking about a radical transformation of consciousness, embraced through an attitude of inner receptivity, a willingness to enter the flow; a commitment to domesticate those violent animal programs within us; and above all, a passionate desire to unify the heart. This is a very powerful fourfold path. It has both a contemporaneity and a timelessness to it—not unlike the teaching you would hear today from the Dali Lama and other great spiritual masters who have dedicated their lives to increasing the quality and quantity of human consciousness."

I am a novice in the ways of the Lord. I continue to strive and to deepen my understanding of what it means to be a spiritual person. Thinking of this book, it could easily have been called *How to Become a Nobody*. All of my life I strived to be someone—a somebody. Now I struggle to be a nobody and to totally empty myself of the ego and its desires. For it is in becoming a nobody that I can be filled with Light. This is the realization of Christ-consciousness.

This entire book speaks of climbing a mountain and gaining greater Light. Think of each beatitude as a rest stop along the slope of the mountain. When we learn the lessons at each stop, we get rid of more of the ego and take on more Light. This illumination allows us to see the world in a different way. This is the gathering of Christ-consciousness that lights our way home.

Chapter Seven

• •

Illumination

"WE SHALL NOT CEASE FROM EXPLORATION AND THE END OF
ALL OUR EXPLORING WILL BE TO ARRIVE WHERE WE STARTED
AND KNOW THE PLACE FOR THE FIRST TIME."
—T. S. Eliot, *The Waste Land, Little Gidding*

To return to the Light—enlightenment—is going Home. It is, however, far from any endpoint. Since we are now speaking of the nonlinear world, there is no possible endpoint—only infinity to ponder.
Like all leaps of consciousness, there is both a horizontal and a vertical
aspect. I think of the horizontal aspect as the taking in of more Light
. . . more information. The vertical journey is the deepening of the
experience both in awareness and understanding. For example, there

are various levels of Samadhi that reveal a deepening of the experience. There is a level in which the aspirant achieves the transcendent only while meditating. There is a deeper and more profound level where the individual persists in the meditative state for some brief time after opening his eyes and ending the meditation practice. The most advanced state is where the devotee lives in a transcendent state and is termed a "sage."

I feel a little foolish trying to write about the experience of, or the resulting state of, enlightenment. It is a nonlinear existence that cannot be described by words. Truth has no words. When I try to put words to an intuitive experience that changes worldview, it is no longer Truth. This is the best I can do. I have prayed for the Presence to work through me in the writing of this book.

Truth is distorted in our Western world. In modern times, we have lost the point of contact. In every ancient culture, life was built around a center of being. This was the point where heaven and earth converge. This is God immanent or the Christ within. With modern civilization, all sense of the sacred, of the transcendent, has disappeared. It is not politically correct or has no scientific validation, we hear. What we are left with is the diagnosis of narcissistic personality disorder and the worship of our own egos.

Then there are those who have been able to see past the allure of the material world. They are walking along the road to personal enlightenment. The narrow road to enlightenment can be long and winding, or it can happen in a flash. It is entirely up to the grace of God. Some, such as the Apostle Paul, reached this state while on a wide road to Damascus. Most, like me, struggled over many lifetimes to learn the lessons necessary in order to find a new life in Jesus Christ.

Enlightenment is a long way from perfection, so one has to continue to strive. There are various degrees of enlightenment as the experience deepens over time. As one continues to grow spiritually, more Light is received. This Light yields a greater understanding of Truth. It was from this gathered Truth or "knowingness" that this book was composed.

In every spiritual tradition, it is known that in order to move closer to the Creator, one has to die. This can be thought of as a threefold experience that spiritual aspirants must go through as a precondition to the enlightened state. These three deaths are death of the world we live in, death of the human body, and finally death of the human ego. All three of these are *maya*—illusions—and they keep us from understanding the Truth, the Absolute. One has to move beyond all three to find Truth.

It is difficult to die to this world of attractions in which we live with all of the fancy gadgets that occupy our time and titillate the ego. Here comes a new operating system, a fancy new car, the next thinnest and fastest smartphone, the latest sex and violence movie thriller, and cable television with its hundreds of stations. With all of this, who has time to do anything else, much less work on their spiritual development? Add to this the almost infinite number of infomercials and ads telling us how to live longer, be sexier, and live healthier if we are only willing to spend the money on their particular product. There is nothing in the material world of great value.

Now we have the human body and especially man's fascination with sex. Sex is exploited in every medium. Today's expression of the perfect female body is supported by whole industries of drugs, surgery, clothing, and makeup. The second death is the demise of the fascination with human flesh, which has no inherent existence. Our fascination with the way we appear to ourselves and others keeps us on a very superficial level. Spiritual growth is about what is beneath the wrapper. To grow spiritually is to grow beyond the world and our bodily image. Because of the unconscious survival value of sex, it is so very difficult to extinguish the passion and desire for the flesh, leading to the character defect of lust. In Matthew 5:28 Jesus states, "But I say to you, that whoever looks at a woman with the desire to covet her, has already committed adultery with her in his heart."

Finally we come to the death of the ego—the most difficult of all. We are speaking of the fascination with the self we call narcissism. This personality that we cultivate is in love with itself and strives to create a personal legacy—to become a somebody. Some want power. Others want a reputation, money, or success. And others want to be great athletes or politicians. We want people to look up to us and we want to feel we are above others and worthy of respect. All of the spiritual paths I have studied diminish the ego by altering the worldview of the spiritual aspirant.

There is truly a paradox involved in the death of the illusions. It is only when we have overcome the world that we can really view its incredible beauty. Only when we have overcome the desire and lust for the human body can we enter into the pure delight of intimacy. Only when the ego is renounced can we discover that which we truly are.

The death of the ego (better understood as ego reintegrated back into its source) leaves a body with a persona that functions in the world. Living from moment to moment, there is a reliance on the Presence to straighten out the highways.

How does one become enlightened? It cannot be acquired, as it is a gift of God. It cannot be reached by reason, as it can only be reached by transcending thought. As long as one is turned toward the five senses and the material world, one will be unable to ascertain the Truth. Once the focus is turned inward toward the Christ within, it can be known by pure intuition. To develop this level of awareness is to know the Truth. As John 8:32 tells us, "And you will know the truth, and that very truth will make you free." With this freedom, there is no more conditioned ego determining the course and decisions of your life.

Enlightenment can be thought of as a transcendent experience. It is an experience of mystical self-transcending. It is also an experience of the Absolute, not so much as an object but as subject. It is a Self that is a "no self," not lacking in anything and living in the moment. There is actually only one Self: God and all of His creation. It is the universal "Oneness." With true transcendence, there is no subject (ego) and object (God); there is no sense of separateness. Any experience where there is still awareness of a separation between Self and God is not enlightenment.

From the Christian perspective, the dynamic of emptying and transcendence defines the transformation into the consciousness of

Christ. It is a kenotic transformation. There is an emptying or surrendering of all of the contents of the ego-consciousness to become an empty vessel. Into this space comes the Light of God to fill the opening with Love. The heart is acknowledged as the center of transformation.

Notice in the religious traditions, the path to transcendence is a path of self-emptying. In Buddhism, for example, the point of highest development of consciousness is when the individual ego is totally emptied and there is identification with the enlightened Buddha. Beware of any path that speaks of self-actualization, self-affirmation, or self-fulfillment, as they lead to a spiritual ego. These are forms of delusion arising out of spiritual ambition that lead to establishing the glory of the ego. This is not transcendence or freedom but the ultimate narcissism.

The way to enlightenment is not that of future progress but a return to Self. There is no forward progress but a constant movement back to that which you are. This is *metanoia* or as the Chinese describes it—a return to the "uncarved block." Remember, Jesus said if you don't become like little children you will never enter the Kingdom of God. Oneness of heart, humility, and meekness—attributes of a child—are necessary to find Truth.

In the Gospel of Thomas, the disciple said to Jesus: "Tell us how our end should be." Jesus said, "Have you then discovered the beginning so that you inquire about the end? For where the beginning is, there shall the end be also."

Figure 7: Arrows

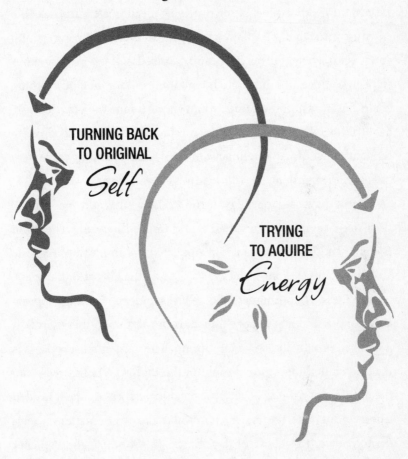

**TURNING BACK
TO ORIGINAL**
Self

**TRYING
TO AQUIRE**
Energy

Figure 7: Moving forward and trying to acquire enlightenment by accumulating energy and information from the world is moving in the wrong direction. This is the method of the ego operating in the material world in which more is better. One must turn back to the original Self—our source. In doing so, we become like a child with a beginner's mind. In Zen, enlightenment is the discovery of the "original face before you were born."

"Transcendence," "Truth," and "metanoia" are all words we use to express the inexpressible. We do not know the ultimate purpose of life as we are incapable of such understanding. It is present in everything and is everywhere, but yet its meaning exceeds our grasp. It is within all things, above all things, and it is all things. Without God, nothing could exist and nothing could be known, yet it remains a mystery. Six centuries before Christ, this is the mystery that Indian and Chinese thought called Atman, Brahman, and Tao—understanding these were only names signifying something mystical and beyond words.

The Buddha said that all is sorrow, all is passing, and all is unreal. Until one faces this head on, there is no awareness of reality. The world is empty and has no authenticity and is *maya*—an illusion. As Bede Griffiths states in *Return to Center*, "This is the horror of darkness, of emptiness, of nothingness, which lurks under all outward appearances of life. To cling to appearances is to court unending sorrow, it is to live perpetually under an illusion. The existentialist today has realized something of this insight of the Buddha. He has seen into the nothingness, the absurdity, the meaninglessness of life. It needed a doctrine of materialism, which mistakes the flux of matter for reality, to recover this sense of the 'vanity' of life, which the Preacher discovered long ago—'Vanity of vanities! All is vanity.'"

In his enlightenment, the Buddha discovered Reality as the not become, unborn, not made, and not compounded, giving an escape from the compounded, made, and born. As Griffiths goes on to say, "This is the mystery. On the one side death, destruction, nothingness, the negation of being, which is maya, the great illusion. But on the other side, where the illusion is seen through, then death itself is found to be eternal life; Siva, the 'destroyer' of the world, is he who re-creates it; the nothingness and the void of Nirvana is the ultimate Truth; the ultimate Reality is not-being rather than being. Did not the great Benedictine monk, Augustine Baker, describe the soul's union with God as 'the union of nothing with Nothing'? For God and the soul are surely not 'things'; to lose one's soul is to save it and even God must die before he can be known for what he is."

In my book *The Ego-Less SELF: Achieving Peace and Tranquility Beyond All Understanding,* I gave testimony to my personal experience of enlightenment. Similar accounts go back thousands upon thousands of years and cross all cultures and religions. I believe this is everyone's destiny as we all are on the path to return to the Light. The Light is our source. I call it God, but many other names suffice. The following is a reprint from pages 14–19 of the last book:

When we have the courage and determination to surrender all to God, the "I," "me," and "mine" of the ego are gone. They are replaced by a persona that lives in this earthly world but is not attached to it. We live for the next world, whatever that might be. The false self of the ego is absorbed into the Self, who sees the essence of things and is not distracted by the egoic notions of comparison and contrast, ownership and personal gain. What remains exists for service to others and sees the world as perfectly just the way God planned it. There is little need for material things, and Madison Avenue marketing doesn't work, because the greed and grandiosity of the ego that fueled it no longer exist. This loss of the ego also rids one of the fear of death, for death is an illusion: only the illusory self can die, since the Self is eternal.

After surrendering everything to God, I experienced incredible anger and rage as my ego sought to stave off its ultimate fate. The ego is very manipulative and is all about survival. There were several people who, because of their lack of integrity, had caused my ego much anger and frustration. The ego raged at these individuals as it fought for its survival as a separate entity. The intensity of the anger was quite shocking to me, as it was far beyond anything I could remember experiencing before. Then, at some point, my body became overwhelmed by severe abdominal pain. After each bout of pain, cramping, and vomiting, the attempt to surrender this agony to God was met with more of the same.

Somewhere in my mind—after a long period of struggling to surrender—I recalled Elisabeth Kübler-Ross's story of enlightenment. In her story, she described an acceptance of her pain. I received the awareness that the ego was not an enemy and could not be surrendered or dispensed with, but must be assimilated into the Self. The ego must be loved into wholeness and thus transformed but not rejected. Love and acceptance of the pain led to instantaneous relief, remarkably with no residual effect, after hours of vomiting and heaving. All was replaced with a sense of calm, and I could finally catch my breath. In this awakened state, I discovered that reality is in essence the glory of the Divine and our true nature is love.

The next twelve hours of my life are difficult to explain. There was no sense of time or place. In the subjective, nonlinear world, there is no time. Christian writers call the experience "mystical union" and the

Vedantists call it "Samadhi" (a superconscious state; the fourth type of consciousness after waking, dreaming, and dreamless sleep). The Bengali mystic Sri Ramakrishna linked the occurrence of Samadhi to the rising of kundalini energy or the "spiritual current." I had been preparing for this experience for a long time, but it was like nothing I could have imagined. My mind was totally overwhelmed by an incredibly powerful energy or infinitely great force that rendered it completely silent. The only event in my life that was even remotely similar was when, as a child, I stood a few feet away from a railroad track and felt the immense power as a train roared by.

The room and everything in it were no longer visible, and the very source of consciousness itself was revealed. All of the beauty of Divinity shone forth, revealing that every breath we take and everything we see, smell, or touch is the language of God. God's radiance was totally consuming and overpowering, yet delightful. Although this experience was incredibly powerful and overwhelming, it was as gentle as a small child. I sensed a connectedness to everything. To say it was stunning is a gross understatement. Everything shimmered, and every movement seemed involuntary and slow. The field of consciousness, what I believe to be the Holy Spirit, was a brilliant white not of this earth. At its core was a mother-of-pearl-like cauldron of energy, and at the periphery was a vibrating, quivering energy without a beginning or end. At first, I was capable of observing this energy field. Later, I would become one with the field, as there was an awareness of nonconceptuality—that is, no difference between subject and object.

At some point, a sense of fear pervaded me as I suddenly had an awareness of evil emanating from the small room next to the one I was in. Then, to my mind came the assertion that "fear is an illusion; walk through it." When I looked directly into the room, I could see an indistinct energy force from my peripheral vision and sensed from it the absence of love. From my "knowingness" came the thought, *Where is the love . . . where is the love of God? I want no part of anything that is absent of God no matter how powerful it might appear.* I am unsure of how I managed to acquire a Bible—perhaps it was an out-of-body experience; perhaps it happened only in my neural structure; perhaps I retrieved it from somewhere—but Psalms 23 and 91 came to me for protection, especially these words from Psalm 91:

Because he has loved me, therefore will I deliver him; I will set him on high because he has known my name. He shall call upon me, and I will answer him; I will be with him in trouble; I will deliver him and honor him. (Psalm 91:14–15, *Holy Bible,* Trans. George M. Lamsa.)

This was the abyss of the void I'd come across so often in my readings—the ultimate duality of "allness" versus nothingness, the ultimate pair of opposites to transcend. The void is infinite but devoid of context. It is absent of God's love. Many have been stuck there. I have read that the void is the last trick up the ego's sleeve. This is a trap even well-known spiritual seekers have fallen into. But the void is an illusion. There is no opposite to the love of God. Allness versus nothingness is a classical duality that, in this instance, needed to be refused—and I did.

Until this point, I had a sense of being able to differentiate myself from the totality of the immense eternal field of vibrating energy. Now the experience intensified, and I was no longer differentiated from the field at all. I was the field, and the field was me. There really was no more *I* or *me*. The suffusion of light and the presence of infinite love with no beginning and no end was undifferentiated from the Self. This was the point where all forms converged into oneness. In the Gospels, Jesus frequently refers to this point as "the light."

All of this happened well over seven years ago. Since that time, there has been a deepening of the experience. I (used in a neutral sense because there is no "I" or "me") find the hunger for spiritual knowledge is still intense, and I still spend hours a day in spiritual study and contemplation. The writing of this book has been my way of consolidating the understanding and growth. Every day, and everything, is new, and the world is a stunningly beautiful place. The first new bit of learning was a shock to me. After thinking I was rid of the ego, I discovered I was somewhat attached to the phenomenon of enlightenment. There was a sense of pride as if I had actually accomplished something. This had to be surrendered, as illumination is a gift from a loving God.

I had not come to a full understanding of the ego and its demise. I believe it is reabsorbed into its source, which is Christ-consciousness or the Self. Since enlightenment doesn't wipe out old memories, the ego comes up as I recall something from the past. It is easy to shed the egoic aspects of this, and it is like experiencing ego functioning in a secondhand way. In regard to old memories, it is as if they are happening in the present. There is little or no distinction in time anymore. If I think of something from forty years ago it is as if it is just occurring. For example, I was thinking of a great friend named Tommy who I lived with in the early seventies. He had just gotten back from Vietnam. My first thought was I needed to get in touch with Tommy only to realize he died of a heroin overdose years ago.

Over the past year, the concept of time has almost completely diminished. If I stayed on our little three acres of land, there would be no time at all other than day and night. Due to an almost constant travel schedule for ten months out of the year, time is hard to escape. There are plane departures, speaking engagements, and so on that make me focus on chronological time, and I wear a watch for the first time in fifteen years. Generally, I am not aware of what day, week, month, or year it is, and I struggle to answer when people ask me how old I am or where I will be next week. However, psychological time and its misery of the past and future is not a part of my mental makeup.

There is no sense of continuity that days, months, and years used to bring about. The vast majority of the time, I am in the moment, going from moment to moment to moment. After a period of adjustment, this has become quite wonderful.

When I am residing in the Presence and letting Christ-consciousness guide my life, there is absolutely no conflict and everything and everyone exists in perfection.

For most of my life I lived for the "highs" and tried to survive the "lows." Now peace is the state of my existence. I do not miss the "highs" and "lows" and am content with my serene existence. I have not had a problem in years.

Emotions can be felt very deeply. I can experience sadness and anger with regard to a situation involving other people, animals, or the environment. Love to one degree or another is always present. All is felt in the moment, so there are no resulting negative judgmental thought patterns such as "I'll get even" to end up in resentments and self-destruction. The world in all of its beauty and depravity is accepted as such. Like you, I try to be of help to others, animals, and the environment when and where I can.

I do not live for this world but for the mystery beyond. The estrangement from this world of illusion is very comfortable. I am not detached but nonattached from this world. Teaching and learning occupy much of my time. It is what I believe I am supposed to be doing, although it could change tomorrow.

As I stated earlier, I do not believe political or social institutions can change this world. My interest is in my and others' spiritual growth. My intention is to be of service whenever possible. It is only when the spiritual consciousness of mankind becomes a more powerful force than the allure of the material world that any true change will take place. If I could capture my present condition in a word it would be *gratitude*. Gratitude occurs in response to the receiving of a gift. The gift of the realization of the Presence has dramatically altered my worldview. Gratitude is a worldview, not a feeling. My worldview doesn't see anything that others cannot see. Due to the fuller realization of the Presence, I view the divinity in all of creation, and the Presence shines forth in all of its glory. A sage sees reality without the distorting lenses of the ego.

Conclusion

"THE TIME WILL COME WHEN THERE ARE NO MAJOR PROBLEMS
IN YOUR OWN LIFE, AND MANY, MANY YEARS GO BY WITHOUT
YOU EVER BEING AWARE OF A MAJOR PROBLEM OF YOUR OWN,
BUT YOU WILL BE DRAWING TO YOU THOSE OF THE WORLD WHO
ARE SEEKING THE SAME FREEDOM THAT YOU HAVE FOUND, AND
YOU WILL BE CALLED UPON TO WORK WITH THEM—TO SERVE,
TO HEAL, AND TO TEACH—BUT ONLY IN PROPORTION TO YOUR
OWN DEMONSTRATION."

—Joel Goldsmith, *The Contemplative Life*

It is a simple certainty that we human beings find it extremely difficult to know the truth about ourselves. In reality, we spend so much
time judging other people and seem to find little or no time to take
an honest look at ourselves. Yet, there is a compulsion within us that
drives us toward the missing factor in our lives. This missing factor
is the Presence of Christ-consciousness that resides in all of us. Realizing this Presence brings truth and the original harmony back into

our lives, allowing us to again experience the "feeling" of a child. We are now in the world but not of it.

If we are to tap into this infinite storehouse called the Presence of Christ-consciousness, if we are to draw to ourselves this infinite good, harmony, perfection, joy, and peace, it is necessary to draw it from within ourselves. There is no acquiring that which we already are and already have. We are all perfect with the only difference between any of us being the level of realization of the Presence.

This is a long and narrow road you have chosen. When you become devoted to the spiritual path, there are elements of your life you have to shrink or totally give up. It takes time and perseverance. I can tell you that for a number of years I withdrew from my family and friends because to discover Truth (or as much of it as God would allow me to discover) was such a driving force that nothing else in my life mattered. I was very willing to die for it although I realized there was no death, but still the transformation is uncertain. As I realized more and more of the Presence, I didn't fit into the material world anymore. The hype didn't work, and material things didn't matter. At times I felt all alone, but as the Presence grew, the boundaries between my life and all other living things diminished. I realized I could never be alone and could never be bored. Here there is no judgment, condemnation, fear, or hatred but a continuous and abiding feeling of forgiveness and love.

In this book, the map I chose is the beatitudes. To study this eight-fold path with discipline and dedication starts with a rigorous honesty born of great humility. It is not so hard to speak of all of your char-acter defects when the defensiveness of pride is diminished and one's humanity is understood. The rigorous journey requires great discipline to stay on the path. During this journey, one has to give up just about everything once thought to be the truth. One must even give up the image of God, as no image is God. As the Presence is realized, one has to get out of the way and let Christ-consciousness both straighten the highway and navigate the journey. While in the moment, acting from the Truth and integrity of the Presence, nothing you do can be wrong. This doesn't mean you will always get what you want but always what you and others need as a result of the actions of the moment.

In his work *Confessions,* the German mystic Jacob Boehme wrote, "For you must realize that earth unfolds its properties and powers in union with Heaven aloft above us, and there is one Heart, one Being, one Will, one God, all in all." Think of two lines intersecting in a perpendicular fashion. The horizontal line represents our relationship with the materialistic world of the ego and its worldview. The vertical line represents the relationship of the true Self (Christ-consciousness) with Heaven—however one conceptualizes this omnipotence—above. When we are active on the horizontal line, our egos flourish and we experience the satisfaction of the ego's desires and the resulting disharmony and conflict it brings. When there is resonance on the vertical axis, we experience the harmony and joy this union begets.

When you realize there is only *one self, one heart, one being,* and *one all in God,* then injustice done to another is injustice done to us all. The highway to a satisfying life is to understand that our neighbor is our self. This leads us to service work, which is the true source of our happiness. We come to the realization that no one on earth has either helped or harmed us. Every offense stemmed from our inability to witness the universe as spiritual and viewing life from the duality of good and evil. Sin, as such, exists but is not real as it results from the false self (ego) and its ignorance of one's true nature. It is what goes out of us that returns to bless or condemn us.

Are we aligning with the vertical axis sending the Love of the Self into the universe or are we attached to the horizontal axis and the greed, prejudice, judgmentalism, and fear of the ego?

In *The Gospel of Mary Magdalene*, Jesus has a "spiritual conversation" (*sobhet*) between Master and students. A *sobhet* is not a didactic exchange of information but is a meeting of minds and hearts where there is energy (Light) transmission from Jesus to His students. The Blessed One stated, "Peace be with you. May my peace reside within you. Guard carefully that no one misleads you saying, 'Look, He is here,' or 'He's over there,' for the Son of Humanity already exists within you. Follow Him, for those who seek Him there will find Him. Go forth, now, and proclaim the Good News concerning the Kingdom. Beyond what I have already given you, do not lay down any further rules nor issue laws as the Lawgiver, lest you too be dominated by them."

I hope this book has been of help to you. I am most grateful and humbled you took the time to read it. If you have questions or comments, I can be reached by email cnuckols@elitecorp1.com.

I wish to leave you with a prayer. This is not just any prayer but a prayer for our nation. It was written by the American Christian evangelist Billy Graham.

"*Heavenly Father, we come before you today to ask your forgiveness and to seek your direction and guidance. We know Your Word says, 'Woe to those who call evil good,' but that is exactly what we have done. We have lost our spiritual equilibrium and reversed our values. We have exploited the poor and called it the lottery. We have rewarded laziness and called it welfare. We have killed our unborn and called it choice. We have shot abortionists and called it justifiable. We have neglected to discipline our children and called it building self-esteem. We have abused power and called it politics. We have coveted our neighbor's possessions and called it ambition. We have polluted the air with profanity and pornography and called it freedom of expression. We have ridiculed the time-honored values of our forefathers and called it enlightenment. Search us, Oh God, and know our hearts today; cleanse us from every sin and Set us free. Amen!*"

As Jesus might say, "Those with ears, hear this."

References

In order of appearance.

Introduction

Griffiths, Bede. *Essential Writings*. Orbis Books Maryknoll, NY, 2004, page 39.

Chapter Two

McTaggart, L. *The Bond*. Free Press, New York, 2011, page 25.

McTaggart, L. *The Bond*. Free Press, New York, 2011, pages xxiv–xxv.

McGee, David. "Smellin' Like a Brewery, Lookin' Like a Tramp," *Rolling Stone* #231 January 27, 1977.

Edward Benton-Banai. *The Mishomis Book (The Voice of the Ojibway)*. University of Minnesota Press, Minneapolis, 1988, page 47.

Chapter Three

Buber, Martin. *I and Thou* (translation by Walter Kaufman). A Touchstone Book, New York, 1970.

Griffiths, Bede. *Return to Center*. Templegate Publishers, Springfield, IL, 1976, pages 113–14.

Chapter Four

Hawkins, David. *The Eye of the I*. Veritas Publishing, Sedona, AZ, 2001, page 65.

DeMello, Anthony. *Awareness*. Image Books, New York, page 91.

Chapter Five

Merton, Thomas. *A Merton Reader, ed.,* Thomas P. McDonnell. New York: Image Books, 1989, page 347.

Thoreau, Henry David. *Walden and Other Writings*. Bantam Books, London, 1950, pages 723–24.

Cassian, John. *The Conferences*. Newman Press, Mahwah, NJ, 1997, page 42.

Griffiths, Bede. *The Cosmic Revelation*. Templegate Publishers, Springfield, IL, 1983, pages 10–11.

Sardello, Robert. *Silence the Mystery of Wholeness*. Goldenstone Press, Benson, NC, 2006, page 1.

Goldsmith, Joel. *The Heart of Mysticism*. Acropolis Books, Santa Barbara, CA, 2007, page 9.

Eddy, Mary Baker. *Science and Health with Key to the Scriptures*. The Christian Science Board of Directors, Boston, MA, 1903, page 9.

Keating, Thomas. *Manifesting God*. Lantern Books, New York, 2005, pages 93–94.

Chapter Six

Griffiths, Bede. *The Cosmic Revelation*. Templegate Publishers, Springfield, IL, 1983, page 41.

Goldsmith, Joel. *Practicing the Presence*. Harper One, New York, 1958, page 15.

Lloyd-Jones, Martyn. *Studies in the Sermon on the Mount*. William B. Eerdmans Publishing Company, Grand Rapids, MI, 1959–60, page 21.

Lloyd-Jones, Martyn. *Studies in the Sermon on the Mount*. William B. Eerdmans Publishing Company, Grand Rapids, MI, 1959–60, page 143.

Segundo, Juan Luis. *The Liberation of Theology*. Orbis Books, Maryknoll, NY, 1976, page 9.

Segundo, Juan Luis. *The Liberation of Theology*. Orbis Books, Maryknoll, NY, 1976, page 9.

Crosby, Michael. *Spirituality and the Beatitudes: Matthew's Vision for the Church in an Unjust World*. Orbis Books, Maryknoll, NY, 2005, pages 43–44.

Lloyd-Jones, Martyn. *Studies in the Sermon on the Mount*. William B. Eerdmans Publishing Company, Grand Rapids, MI, 1959–60, page 41.

Lloyd-Jones, Martyn. *Studies in the Sermon on the Mount*. William B. Eerdmans Publishing Company, Grand Rapids, MI, 1959–60, page 50–51.

MacArthur, John. *The Beatitudes: The Only Way to Happiness*. Moody Publishers, Chicago, IL, 1980, pages 112–13.

MacArthur, John. *The Beatitudes: The Only Way to Happiness*. Moody Publishers, Chicago, IL, 1980, pages 133–34.

Fox, Emmet. *The Sermon on the Mount*. Harper Collins, New York, 1989, pages 38–39.

MacArthur, John. *The Beatitudes: The Only Way to Happiness*. Moody Publishers, Chicago, IL, 1980, pages 168–69.

Lloyd-Jones, Martyn. *Studies in the Sermon on the Mount*. William B. Eerdmans Publishing Company, Grand Rapids, MI, 1959–60, page 118.

Lloyd-Jones, Martyn. *Studies in the Sermon on the Mount*. William B. Eerdmans Publishing Company, Grand Rapids, MI, 1959–60, page 122.

Bourgeault, Cynthia. *The Wisdom Jesus*. Shambhala, Boston, MA, 2008, page 47.

Chapter Seven

Eliot, T. S., *The Waste Land, Little Gidding*, Four Quartets, 1943.

Griffiths, Bede. *Return to Center*. Templegate Publishers, Springfield, IL, 1976, page 21.

Griffiths, Bede. *Return to Center*. Templegate Publishers, Springfield, IL, 1976, pages 22–23.

Conclusion

Goldsmith, Joel. *The Contemplative Life*. Martino Publishing, Mansfield Centre, CT, 2010, page 85.

Boehme, Jacob, *Confessions*. Kessinger, Kila, MT: n.d., page 41.

Bourgeault, Cynthia. *The Meaning of Mary Magdalene*. Shambhala Publications, Boston, MA, 2010, page 47.

Recommended Reading

Armour, JA. *Neurocardiology: Anatomical and Functional Principles*. Oxford University Press, New York, 1994.

Blofeld, John. *The Zen Teachings of Huang Po*. Grove Press, New York, 1958.

Bourgeault, Cynthia. *Centering Prayer and Inner Awakening*. Cowley Publications, Latham, MD, 2004.

Bourgeault, Cynthia. *The Wisdom Jesus*. Shambhala, Boston, MA. 2008.

Cassian, John. *The Conferences*. Newman Press, New York, 1997.

Childre, D., and McCraty, R. "Psychophysiological Correlates of Spiritual Experience," *Biofeedback* 29(4), 2001, pages 13–17.

Lloyd-Jones, Martyn. *Studies in the Sermon on the Mount*. William B. Eerdmans Publishing Company, Grand Rapids, MI, 1959–60.

De Mello, Anthony. *"Awareness."* Image Books, New York, 1990.

De Mello, Anthony. *"The Heart of Enlightenment."* Image Books, New York, 1991.

De Mello, Anthony. *"The Way to Love."* Image Books, New York, 1991.

Goldsmith, Joel. *A Parenthesis in Eternity*. Harper One, New York, 1963.

Goldsmith, Joel. *Living the Infinite Way*. Acropolis Books, Santa Barbara, CA, 1961.

Goldsmith, Joel. *Practicing the Presence*. Harper One, New York, 1958.

Goldsmith, Joel. *The Art of Meditation*. Harper One, New York, 1956.

Goldsmith, Joel. *The Infinite Way*. DeVorss Publications, Camarillo, CA, 1947.

Goldsmith, Joel. *The Thunder of Silence*. Harper One, New York, 1961.

Griffiths, Bede. *Essential Writings*. Orbis Books, New York, 2004.

Griffiths, Bede. *Return to Center*. Templegate Publishers, Springfield, IL, 1976.

Griffiths, Bede. *The Cosmic Revelation*. Templegate Publishers, Springfield, IL, 1983.

Holy Bible from the Ancient Eastern Test (George Lamsa's translation), Harper, San Francisco, 1961.

Krishnamurti, J. *Life Ahead: On Learning and the Search for Meaning*. New World Library, Novato, CA, 1963

Krishnamurti, J. *Meeting Life*. Harper One, New York, 1991.

Krishnamurti, J. *On God*. Harper One, New York, 1992.

Krishnamurti, J. *On Love and Loneliness*. Harper One, New York, 1993.

Krishnamurti, J. *To Be Human*. Shambala Publications, Boston, MA, 2000.

Lorimer, D. *Thinking Beyond the Brain: A Wider Science of Consciousness*. Floris Books, Edinburg, UK, 2001.

McArthur, John. *The Beatitudes: The Only Way to Happiness*. Moody Publishers, Chicago, IL, 1980.

McCraty, R., Atkinson, M., and Bradley, R.T. "Electrophysiological Evidence of Intuition: Part 1. The Surprising Role of the Heart," *Journal of Alternative and Complementary Medicine* 10(1): 2004, pages 133–143. (see also Part 2 10(2), pages 325–336).

Merton, Thomas. *Zen and the Birds of Appetite*. New Directions Book, New York, 1968.

Merton, Thomas. *A Book of Hours*. Sorin Books, Notre Dame, IN, 2007.

Moss, Richard. *The Mandala of Being*. New World Library, Novato, CA, 2007.

Nouwen, Henri. *The Way of the Heart*. Ballantine Books, New York, 1981.

Pearce, T. Chilton. *The Biology of Transcendence*. Kindle Books.

Radin, D. *The Conscious Universe: The Scientific Truth of Psychic Phenomenon*. Harper Edge, San Francisco, 1997.

Sanford, John. *Mystical Christianity*. The Crossroad Publishing Co., New York, 1993.

Shankara, *Crest-Jewel of Discrimination*. Vedanta Press, Hollywood, CA., 1975.

The Cloud of Unknowing. Penguin Books, London, England, 2001.

Vyasa. *The Bhagavad Gita*. Borders Classics, Ann Arbor, MI, 2007.

About the Author

Dr. Cardwell C. Nuckols has been described as "one of the most influential teachers in North America." His passion and mission is to assist in the integration of emerging scientific research with traditional spiritual wisdom. His professional background includes advanced work in pharmacology, neurobiology, education, and psychology. His personal spiritual path involves studies of various spiritual traditions, including early contemplative Christianity. This journey has led him to the very rare, illuminated state of "enlightenment."

Dr. Nuckols conducts workshops and spiritual retreats throughout the UnitedStates and other nations. He can be reached by e-mail at cnuckols@elitecorp.org or visitwww.cnuckols.com.

Products available at www.cnuckols.com

Discovery to Recovery (CD and DVD)

Psychology, Spirituality and True Happiness (CD and DVD)

Removing Defects of Character (CD and DVD)

The Art and Science of Healing (CD and DVD)

The Ego-Less Self: Achieving Peace & Tranquility Beyond All Understanding (Book)